Stories from a Theme Park Insider

Robert Niles

Text Copyright © 2011 by Robert Niles
Illustrations are Copyright © 2011 by Laurie Niles

Published by Niles Online
315 South Sierra Madre Boulevard, Suite C
Pasadena, CA 91107

ISBN: 978-0-9838130-1-9

A hearty thank you to all the people, past and present, who make the magic at the world's theme parks. And to the readers who love them for that.

Contents

Foreword

My wife, Laurie, and I went out for dinner one night in Austin, Texas, with a mutual friend from college, who'd married a lawyer from Argentina.

They're fluent in Spanish, so Laurie was practicing her *Español*, as she likes to do with native and fluent speakers. Our friend asked if I knew Spanish, too, and I replied that I know a few phrases.

Laurie rolled her eyes. "Go ahead," she said. So I rattled off my best Spanish, as our friend arched her eyebrow higher with each phrase:

"Cuatro personas por fila, por favor."[1]

"No más de veinticuatro personas por barco."[2]

"Permanezcan sentados, por favor."[3]

"Mantenga las manos y los brazos dentro del barco."[4]

"No tomar fotografías con flash."[5]

I could tell she was struggling to find some context for these seemingly random phrases, but her blank stare turned to understanding once Laurie explained....

"He learned to speak Spanish working at Pirates of the Caribbean."

---

[1] "Four people per row, please"

[2] "No more than 24 people per boat"

[3] "Remain seated, please"

[4] "Keep your hands and arms inside the boat"

[5] "No flash photography"

Years earlier, as I was finishing wrapping up my senior year at Northwestern University, some of my classmates were planning to head off to Europe before settling down to their post-graduation jobs. I would have loved to go to Europe and see more of the world, too. But I went to school on a Pell Grant and more than once had to hunt coins on the floor to pay for a fast-food Sunday dinner (when the cafeterias were closed). No way could a kid like me afford a European tour.

Well, if I couldn't afford to go out and see the world, I knew where to get a job where the world would come see me: Walt Disney World's Magic Kingdom. As soon as my classes were over, I crammed my belongings into two pieces of luggage and couple cardboard boxes, and I hopped a flight for Orlando.

While my classmates were sitting in Northwestern's basketball arena a week later, collecting their diplomas, I was standing in the theater at the Country Bear Vacation Hoedown, trying to elicit a rowdy "Howdy" from several platoons of Brazilian teen-agers.

Working at the world's most popular theme park off and on for five years not only puts you face-to-face with tourists from all over the world, it lets you meet some of the world's most famous people. Heads of state. Hollywood actors. When Michael Jackson died and my kids were talking about him, they were shocked when I told them that I once had met the singer. Jackson and his crew had boarded my boat at Pirates of the Caribbean.

Still, the "regular" guests stand out as much as the celebrities. One day, while walking Tom Sawyer Island, I heard a whoop from two middle-aged British ladies. When I walked over to see what was the matter, they begged me to take their picture next to the "Cardiff Hill" sign on the island.

They told me that they'd been trying to find a shortcut from Thunder Mountain to the Haunted Mansion. But they'd gotten themselves royally lost on what they still hadn't realized was, as the name said, an island. Yet their hopeless frustration had melted away and now they were thrilled. Why? They were from the city of Cardiff, in Wales, and were delighted to find a sign referencing their hometown in the Magic Kingdom.

I took their picture with the sign, shared a laugh, and walked them back to the dock for a return trip to the mainland. (I told them how to get over to the Mansion, too.)

Funny how things work out. They'd been looking for one thing, but gotten themselves good and lost. Only then could they find that thing they hadn't known about, something that ended up making their trip. They had traveled across an ocean – to find a delightful reminder of home.

The same thing happened to me. I thought working at a theme park would be time off, a diversion from my future career in journalism. Little did I know that within a generation, the newspaper industry would self-destruct, and that as hundreds of former colleagues lost their jobs, I would remain employed in journalism as... the editor of a website covering theme parks.

In 1999 I founded ThemeParkInsider.com, and since then I have offered advice, collected readers' ratings and reviews, hosted discussions, advocated for theme park safety and kept on top of theme park news as the editor of the website. In this book I have collected some my stories from working at the Walt Disney World Resort, stories which originally appeared on ThemeParkInsider.com as a series called "Theme Park Cast Member Stories." Often, readers responded with their own stories, some of which I have included in this book, too.

So I didn't take a year off back when I worked at Disney, after all. I was starting a career that I didn't yet know I'd have.

Funny how things work out.

Smile if you want to work for a theme park

July 1987 - Less than two miles from the world's most popular theme park, and I'm in the middle of nowhere.

Orange groves, in every direction, as far as I can see. A deep blue sky overhead, with no clouds to shade Central Florida's brutal summer sun. The temperature's already well past 90, and so's the humidity, even at 9 a.m. I slow my car as the intersection approaches. There's no light, no big sign. Just a narrow pole with a street name perched on top. Reams Road. As I turn the wheel to the left, a dusty old sedan blasts from the road, peeling around the corner to the right, speeding off in the direction I'd just come.

A little over a mile down the road, I pull up to a set of mobile home-style trailers. "Casting," the sign says, with a small, hyper-enthusiastic Mickey Mouse painted beside.

Welcome to the back side of Walt Disney World.

My parents had moved to Orlando the previous fall while I was attending Northwestern University, north of Chicago. Not having anywhere else to go for the summer, I followed them down to Orlando, hoping I could find a gig when I arrived.

1

Northwestern breaks for the summer in mid-June, which can make it tough to find a decent summer job. Most of the good ones get snapped up a month earlier by the students who get out in May. But my sister, who was still in high school, had landed a job in the foods department in the Magic Kingdom, so I figured I'd give Disney a shot, too.

The fact that I knew only one other employer in town probably influenced that decision, too. (If I didn't get the Disney job, my plan was to drive over to SeaWorld and try my luck there. Shamu, I could have worked for you!)

I'd called Disney for an appointment, but they told me to just come on in. So I did, walking up to a lady in a sundress who was sitting behind the desk in the cramped trailer. I asked for an application.

Yes, here you go. Fill it out, please. Take a seat, please. We'll call you back for an interview in a few moments, thank you.

Twenty minutes later, three of us were called into another trailer, two young ladies around my age and me.

Since all the workers seems to have had wide grins plastered onto their faces, I figured I should put on my chipper happy face, too. I walked in with a big smile and tried to be as enthusiastic as I possibly could about any job with the Walt Disney World Resort, all the while hoping that I wouldn't get stuck in foods like my little sister. Or worse, custodial.

One of the two girls matched my fake enthusiasm, smile for smile. We shot each other sarcastic looks whenever the interviewer looked away from us, and suppressed giggles as if to say, "I cannot believe we're acting this silly." But we just ratcheted our enthusiasm up another notch each time the interviewer looked back at us.

The second girl answered her questions politely, with a pleasant, yet professional, expression on her face. No corny smiles. When the interviewer looked away from her, she'd shoot the two of us a disapproving schoolmarm glare, to silently reproach us for not being professional enough in a job interview. She reminded me of my classmates at Northwestern - the serious ones, headed to Europe before starting their lives on Wall Street.

Later I learned that the first girl was a relative of a then-nationally-famous Republican politician, so she'd been around political campaigns her entire life. She certainly knew how to turn on the charm. I talked with her again on our first day as "cast members," as Disney calls its employees. We were working the cash registers at the old Mickey's Mart souvenir shop in Tomorrowland.

The second girl? I never saw her again. She didn't get the gig.

Years later, a person who's been around the theme park business for years told me about the interview form used by another theme park chain. It contained nothing but six empty checkboxes.

The interviewer would make up whatever questions he or she wanted to ask the applicants. The applicant's answers didn't matter. The interviewer would simply check one of the boxes whenever the applicant smiled.

If the applicant smiled six times before the interview was over, he or she got a job. Those who didn't smile enough didn't get hired - no matter what they said, where they went to school or where they'd worked before.

So if you've ever thought about working for The Mouse, or any other theme park, I have just one piece of advice for you.

Smile. A lot.

Tunnel vision

Getting to work in the Magic Kingdom is as much an ordeal as getting into the park as a paying customer. As a "guest," as Disney likes to call its visitors, you park miles away from the Magic Kingdom then ride over across a vast man-made lake, via sleek monorails or massive ferryboats.

Working at the Magic Kingdom, you also park miles away, but it's a bus that hauls you from the parking lot to the theme park. And you don't enter the park by walking underneath a turn-of-the-20th-century steam-train station. Instead, you enter the gaping maw of the no-they're-not-an-urban-legend Magic Kingdom tunnels.

Why tunnels? Company lore said that Walt wasn't happy when Disneyland workers walked across the park to get to their jobs, passing through themed "lands" where their costumes didn't match.

Disney dresses its theme park employees in costumes themed to the specific location where they work. Attendants at The Hall of Presidents are dressed like the just stepped through a time machine from 1776. Workers at Big Thunder Mountain Railroad are dressed like Old West silver miners (assuming the silver mine was located in The Castro). People who work in Tomorrowland were dressed as if they worked in a future where the cotton plant was extinct.

The solution to Walt's problem? Tunnels. Workers would walk from location to location in the park through underground tunnels, emerging like prairie dogs from a hole at their assigned workplace. Since Walt chose to build his World atop a giant swamp, the company couldn't dig underground. Instead, it built its tunnels as corridors atop the ground, then dug up a giant "lake" in front them and buried the corridors under all that dirt.

Voila. "Tunnels." So when you're visiting the Magic Kingdom, you're actually walking on the second floor of the park's structure. Underneath lies the passageways, dressing rooms, stockrooms, employees cafeterias, technical control rooms and garbage chutes that betray the "Magic Kingdom" as a giant factory where amusement's the product.

Dozens of employees walk together through the long, curving tunnels, all clad in the same costume (as Disney refers to all work uniforms). Sometimes, giant "rubberhead" costumed characters would accompany them. Electric carts scoot down the passageways, carefully steering around the costumed crowds. The tunnels might be a factory, but they look more like the corridors of a Disneyified Death Star.

Custodians shovel trash into rooms the size of your kitchen, which open into vast AVAC (automated vacuum collection) tubes that suck the garbage from every corner of the Kingdom at 60 miles per hour. While on their breaks, cast members line up for discount food in the cafeteria, where the most expensive item when I worked there was the prime rib dinner, offered for $4.95 every Thursday. (Thursday, not coincidentally, was payday. The company giveth. The company taketh away.)

You can create the illusion of perfection up above, but you never can eliminate the infrastructure - the labor, the mess - that supports any effort. At most, you can bury it.

At at the mouth of the tunnel, you find the costume department and dressing rooms, where Disney's ever-friendly "cast members" morph back into normal, and even snarky and sarcastic, Central Floridians. I remember one thin young blonde, with dimpled cheeks and a button nose, emerging from the ladies' dressing room wearing a T-shirt from her college: the University of South Carolina. On the front was a picture of the school's gamecock mascot. On the back?

This: "The University of South Carolina. The *Real* USC. What good is a Trojan without a Cock?"

Yeah, you're in the tunnels now.

Boozy McTourist and the Giant Stuffed Mouse

My first assignments as a cast member at the Magic Kingdom was at the cash register at Mickey's Mart.

Mickey's Mart was one of the largest stores in the Magic Kingdom, second only to Main Street's Emporium in sales, I was told. Despite the faux-futuristic Tomorrowland location, the merchandise was pretty much the standard Disney theme park fare - shirts, plush toys, candy, even cigarettes under the counter. (But no gum - no one on Disney property could sell chewing gum. You wanna clean up that gunk?)

The biggest item in the store was an enormous stuffed Mickey Mouse, perched on a ledge under the store's ceiling, opposite the big observation windows where the People Mover ride drove past, showing off the souvenir shop to all the tourists who might still yet have some money in their wallets.

This Mickey stood close to five feet tall, and cost around $300, if memory serves. Mickey was graying with age, thanks to a growing layer of dust. Surely no out-of-town tourist would be fool enough to buy something so big. If one did, I was told, there was a second Gi-nor-Mouse waiting backstage, since it'd be too much hassle to move the Big Mick from his perch.

One late July evening, just after the fireworks and about an hour before closing, a middle-aged man stumbled up to the register next to mine, and bellowed, waving toward Big Mickey, "How much for that Mickey Mouse up there?"

This was not an uncommon question, as tourists often gawked at the Big Guy.

"That Mickey is $300," the cast member next to me replied. That usually sent the tourists on their way.

"I'll take it," he belched.

Stunned silence. Every cast member in the room, it seemed, plus a whole lot of tourists, turned to look at the guy.

One of those onlookers was the man's daughter, who appeared to be in her mid-teens... and looking very forward to the day when she wouldn't have to be seen in public with her dad ever again.

"No way, Dad. You can't buy that. We'd never get it home," she protested, trying to hide under her bangs to avoid all the strangers' eyes.

"Hah," Dad cut across her. "You wanted a Mickey Mouse. I'm going buy you a Mickey Mouse."

She looked like she'd prefer evaporating on the spot, but Dad was getting his way. As he handed over his American Express card, both the cast member taking his card and I got a whiff of the booze Dad had been drinking.

Hey, many of us had joked that the only way someone would be fool enough to buy Big Mick would be if they were drunk. But given that the Magic Kingdom didn't serve alcohol, we figured someone would need to have gotten pretty loaded at Epcot or the hotels to make it all the way back to the Magic Kingdom and still be buzzed enough to do the deal.

Well, that night, Boozy McTourist came through.

Of course, it took a while to explain to Boozy that he wasn't getting *that* Mickey, but a clean one we'd stored backstage. And that he couldn't just carry something that large from the store, that he'd have to pick it up at the park exit, where we would deliver it. As we explained all this, I could see the slosh in his expression turning to stupor... and his daughter's embarrassment mutating into an anger that I am sure would fuel many therapy sessions in the years to come.

Backstage, the stock guys were fighting over who got to drive Mickey on the service cart through the park's underground service tunnels to the Main Street entrance, where hosts at the merchandise pick-up location already were gleefully awaiting Boozy McTourist's arrival. I never did hear what happened there, but the next night, there was another Big Mick waiting backstage, for the next drunken tourist with too much money and a child to embarrass.

The Mouse is always watching

You'd think that working in a place called Tomorrowland, Disney's stores would have employed the latest retail technology.

If you believe that, you might also believe they had real cowboys and Indians over in Frontierland.

Not so. In the summer of 1987, while mall stores had new-fangled things like magnetic stripe readers to charge credit cards, we were still processing cards with carbon imprints. (Google it, kids!) To see if a card was valid, we had to look for the number in a printed booklet of lost and fraudulent card numbers.

And we thought we had it lucky. In the other stores in Tomorrowland, checkers were still using old manual cash registers, ones that did not have electronic displays, but little pop-up metal digits. To compute the sales tax, you had to read the "fine print" numbers on the bottom of each digit, add them across in your head, and then add that amount to the register's total.

Tomorrowland? Try Hooterville.

While Disney hadn't yet coughed up the dough for modern cash registers, it spared no expense on security. The Brazilian with the $50 bill taught me that.

The man stood across the counter, smiling under his red baseball cap, as he handed me what he thought was a $50 bill.

The guy's kids, waiting on either side of him, eyeing their new souvenirs, probably could have drawn a better fake with a green Crayola. This was, literally, a two-sided photocopy of a $50 bill. In black and white. The guest didn't speak a word of English. He'd likely never seen a real U.S. $50 bill before and didn't know any better.

Standard operation procedure when accepting a bill of $50 or larger was to show it under the counter to the checker next to you, to confirm the bill wasn't a fake. In this case, there was no doubt. I hiked an eyebrow as I held out the fake to my co-worker, who hiked both of his in return, then excused himself to his customer to quietly dial the supervisor's office on the phone next to his register.

Moving as slowly as a lost tourist driving a rental car on Interstate 4, I took my time making change for my customer, trying to stall while my co-worker made the call. When he returned, he told me to finish the sale and close up for an immediate "break."

I tried to keep my eye on the customer as I walked around the counter, toward the store's back office. But before I could walk five steps, a large man in sunglasses grabbed me by the shoulder.

"Come with me," he said, as I broke eye contact and lost sight of Mr. Fakebucks and family.

The man pulled a walkie-talkie from his pants pocket and muttered, "I'm with the checker."

Sixty seconds hadn't passed from the moment Fakebucks passed me the bill, and Disney's Security Guy already was on the scene. He told me to take off my name tag and walk with him around the area while we looked for Fakebucks and family.

Three minutes later, I found them, standing under the Astro Orbiter platform, wearing his red baseball cap and holding his crisp new Disney shopping bag. Security Guy muttered something else into his walkie-talkie, then grabbed me again by the shoulder, pulling me away. As I looked back over my shoulder, I saw two more Disney Security Guys converging on the Fakebuck family.

Thirty minutes and about 500 forms later, I saw the Facebucks family in a small conference room in the tunnels under Main Street, when Senior Security Guy brought me in to ID the suspect. Mrs. Fakebucks saw me, pointed, and called out what sounded like "the man from the store" in what was probably Portuguese but sounded close enough to Spanish for me to understand. Senior Security Guy hustled me away.

He then explained that Mr. Fakebucks was a journalist from Brasilia. He'd bought the fake money in a marketplace in Brazil, thinking he was getting real American bills. He was as much a victim as Disney, which was letting him go. The fake money would go to the Secret Service, along with whatever information Fakebucks could give about where he'd bought the phony cash.

"Hey, this happens every day here," Senior Security Guy told me, pointing at a locker filled with fake cash, awaiting delivery to the Secret Service.

So how was Security Guy able to get to me so fast?

"When your store called it in, we radioed the undercover in the area," he explained. "We always have a plainclothes agent in or around the major stores in the park," he bragged.

So there you go. Wherever you go at Disney, Mickey's always watching you.

Don't mess with the Mouse.

A *reader responds:*

When I was 19 years old, I was recruited to work in the best job at Walt Disney World: Blessed with a youthful appearance and boyish good looks, on three occasions, for one week periods, I worked in internal security as a Walt Disney World shopper.

I was a college student, and at the time the drinking age in Florida was 19. When I arrived, I was introduced to my boss, an older, rubber-faced mook by the name of Joe. Joe was friendly enough. He had come to Disney by way of the Philadelphia Police Department. His old job (and I swear this part is true): Homicide.

"I like working for Disney," he told me. "It's nicer dealing with people who are still alive."

We sat in a small conference room, where Joe laid out the job. My partner and I were assigned to visit the bars, order a drink, toss it back, pay for the drink, then come outside and report whether or not the server had checked our IDs.

"I don't want to get anyone fired," my partner said.

Joe shook his head and waved his hands. "No, no. They can't get fired. You two are both 19. It's legal to sell you alcohol. This program works because it seems every time a bartender or server gets a warning, they never let a younger-looking guest slip by them again. What we're doing is preventing any kid who is actually underage from getting his hands on a cocktail. And we can't send underage kids in to order drinks, because we would be accused of dressing them up or making them up to look older."

I nodded at the girl. "I'm in!"

So for the next five days, we romped around Disney World getting liquored up. And (like I said) it was the best Disney job ever! Disney paid for the booze. And they paid me by the hour to do the "work."

They had to keep food in our stomachs, or we would have been completely schwacked in under three hours. Disney paid for the food. During the three times I worked in the program over a year, I ate at virtually all of the restaurants on the property. During my second stint, I got eight hours *overtime* to attend one of the Sunday champagne brunches.

At the end of the workday, you filled out some reports. Everyone in the security office knew what our assignment had been. So they were always goofing on us ("How many fingers am I holding up?" "Walk this straight line.")

But, bringing this around to the original topic, it was on a busy December afternoon, after I did my last turn as a shopper, that I was in the Magic Kingdom. It was after Christmas, and the park was crowded with people who wanted to see the Holiday Parade. While walking along Main Street, I spotted Joe. I walked over, shook his hand and wished him a Happy New Year. As I moved on, out of the corner of my eye, I spotted another plainclothes internal security officer that I had met from the job, and not too far down the street, I saw a third.

The Mouse really is always watching.

'Is that *really* your name?'

My favorite place to work in the Magic Kingdom was Tom Sawyer Island, driving the rafts to and from the island, which I learned to do the next summer. One day there, though, the glue holding my name tag to the pin attaching it to my shirt gave way in the sticky Florida heat, and the tag dropped into the river.

No big deal; just take the pin back downstairs to the costume department, and they'll give you another one, free. (They'd charge you a buck for the lost tag if you didn't have the pin and the story, but I did.)

The quickest way to get a new tag was to check the bin with spare name tags on the counter. If you found one with your first name on it, great. Grab it and go. If not, you'd have to wait a few days for them to make you a new tag. In the meantime, you'd borrow one of the spares. Unfortunately, that meant that you would have to go by that other name while "on stage" in the park until your new tag arrived.

No "Robert." I'm out of luck. Anything else that starts with an "R"?

Let's see. Robin? No. Too many people will think that's a girl's name. Roger? No, I work with one and don't want people to get confused about who's who.

Wait, could this be? You're kidding. No... this is perfect!

Randy.

"Randy" is a pretty normal name in America, a nice nickname for "Randall." However, for the British, it's rather like if a person named "Horace" picked a tag with the unfortunate, nickname of "Horny."

Unfortunate, but wildly hilarious.

The park was crawling with British tourists that week. I imagined the fuss my fake name tag would create. Lovely young English ladies would cozy up to me, while their boyfriends would look on jealously, knowing that they couldn't possibly be as "randy" as me.

I walked up to my shift at the Swiss Family Treehouse with the "Yakkity Sax" theme playing in my head, imagining the day to unfold like a Benny Hill episode.

"Is that *really* your name?" I heard moments later, in an unmistakable English accent.

"Yes, ma'am, it is," I lied, like a good Disney cast member. Smiling, I turned my head, expecting to see a fetching young Bond girl, but seeing instead an elderly lady who looked like Miss Marple's grandmother.

She grabbed her friend by the arm.

"You've got to take a look at this!" she exclaimed, pulling her equally gray and wrinkled friend toward me.

"I have got to get a picture!" the first granny squealed, wrapping her arm around me, cutting the air to my lungs. She threw her camera toward her friend.

Granny number two wasn't going to be left out. She chucked the camera at the next person in line and squeezed in on the other side of me. The second lady wasn't anywhere near my height, so when she wrapped her arm around my waist, it barely cleared my rear end. I ground my teeth and prayed that the other guest would finish snapping the picture before her arm dropped any lower.

"Wait 'til we tell the others about this!" the second lady giggled.

Oh, dear Lord, no.

They each winked at me as they walked away, giggling to each other. And, sure enough, minutes later another group of retirees approached the Treehouse entrance, chattering among themselves like an embarrassed group of tweenagers. For the rest of my shift, I posed with more elderly English women than Mickey Mouse did with kids that day.

I was never happier at Disney than I was when I finally got my "Robert" name tag back.

A reader replies:

I was a Walt Disney World College Program participant back in spring 2008, and I was assigned to Kali River Rapids at Disney's Animal Kingdom. It was around early March, so if you've ever worked at Disney, you know that's the time when all the cheerleaders are rumbling around the parks while not at their annual competition. It was a Wednesday, which meant we had our evening "Extra Tragic Hours," oh, I mean "Extra Magic Hours," and nobody was on our ride. Half way through, there was a big group of cheerleaders, about 16 years of age.

Oh boy...here comes trouble...

They took up three rafts, back to back to back. I was the only loader on the turntable at the time, so I had the "privilege" of loading each one on to the rafts. At this point I should mention I had forgotten my name tag, so I had to grab another name tag that morning. Today was my lucky day...that day I was the gender-inappropriate "Marge."

Continuing my story, I was going through my spiel to buckle up and put all belongings in the center console, yada yada yada. Well, one girl was yelling, "Marge, Marge!"...and I didn't think anything of it, thinking that somebody in the raft was named Marge. But she kept yelling "Marge!" I completely forgot that I was wearing that name tag, and I was "Marge." So when we made eye contact, I started to laugh and told them that wasn't my real name. She asked what my real name was, and playing along and trying to make small talk, I asked, "What do you think my name is? Guess." She looked me over and...here it comes...she yells:

"You look like a McLovin!"

Now I know what you're thinking...yes, I am a tall, skinny, white kid, but I don't really think of myself as a McLovin build. Anyway, everybody in the raft busted out laughing. The girl yelled to the other rafts, "Hey! Doesn't he look like McLovin?" And now everybody was giggling; even my fellow cast members were laughing. So they went on their merry way, and we waited for them to complete their journey.

When they got back, the girls in the rafts were yelling, "Hey McLovin!" and, "We love you, McLovin!" Taking advantage of this situation, I raised my arms and told them to yell louder. Since nobody was in line, they decided to go again. So they left again, then five minutes later they came back around, roaring even louder, "McLovin!" I played along, jumping on their rafts and egging them on. They left once more, and my fellow cast members and I were convinced they'd get tired of the whole McLovin routine, get cold and tired of the ride, and get off.

We were wrong.

As they rounded the corner, coming back to the turntable, we all stopped. "What's that sound?" asked one cast member, "Do you hear that?" Well, in the three or four minutes during the ride, the cheerleaders had come up with – what else -- a cheer:

"We're ready! We're ready! We're ready...for McLOVIN!"

Just as they were coming back to the station, our manager came down to the turntable with a confused look on his face. I could only stand there and shrug as these young cheerleaders chanted my fictitious name.

So from then on, through the rest of my time at Disney, I was known throughout all of Animal Kingdom as "The Infamous McLovin."

The stroller police

Ever leave a stroller outside a Walt Disney World attraction, only to find it in a different place when you returned?

You might have been a target of the Disney Stroller Police.

Yeah, I served on the force. People curse our work, but trust me, you don't want to try walking through a theme park without the Stroller Police there to clear the way.

When you work at a theme park attraction, one of your responsibilities is to keep the area around the entrance clean and orderly. So when people pull their kids from their strollers before coming inside, we follow behind and move those strollers into neat lines.

Once we establish the stroller parking zone in the morning, most people follow along, parking their strollers at the end of the rows, or filling a space left empty by a previous visitor.

But some never do get the hint. They leave the stroller wherever their child gets out, completely unconcerned that it's blocking a pathway, or an exit door, or even someone else's stroller. So we stroller cops grab it and push it into the proper place.

It turns out that most sloppy stroller parkers never complain. I suspect they don't pay any attention to where they've left the stroller; they just assume they'll find it somewhere in the line-up of the strollers in front of the attraction when they exit. To them, the stroller police are more like stroller valets.

But these are only minor stroller parking infractions. Let's talk about the real stroller felons:

The pack rats

These folks pack for a day at Disney World as if they were hauling their kids across the country on a six-month backpacking trek. The over-worn wheels of their top-heavy strollers barely roll as they try to wrestle the mess into place. I could understand why you might want to bring half the contents of your children's bedroom to entertain them if you were spending the afternoon waiting in line at the Department of Motor Vehicles. But this is Disney World, people. We've got plenty here to keep your children entertained.

Stinky the Stroller

Disney World is not a backcountry campsite. You don't need to pack out everything you brought in. It's okay to dump your soiled diapers in the bathroom someplace. You don't need to haul them around the park with you all day. Okay?

I couldn't afford a Ferrari, so I bought this stroller instead

Dad - and it is always Dad - charges toward the nearest cast member, pointing at his Deluxe, Top-of-the-Line Stroller Machine: "Hey, this is a very expensive stroller," he says. "I know you guys are supposed to move the strollers around, but as you can see, we parked it in an okay place. I really don't want anyone touching it, okay?" Then he storms off, running after his family, who have hurried into the attraction queue early to enjoy a moment away from Daddy-with-issues. Of course, half the time Mr. Wonderful hasn't parked the stroller in "an okay place." But even if he has, he deserves something for his little performance. No, we won't move his precious Ferrari substitute. But wouldn't it look even more impressive with a Stinky the Stroller parked next to it?

Now for the worst of the stroller felons:

The lockers

Incredibly, some people are so afraid their strollers will be stolen, or even relocated, that they lock them to stanchions, lampposts or fences. If you do this far enough away from the attraction, we might not notice. But when the Stroller Police see a locked stroller blocking an exit door or pathway next to an attraction, we call out the Stroller SWAT Team.

I only saw the Stroller SWAT Team in action once. Someone had locked a pack-rat stroller (ooh, a multiple offender!) to a lamppost outside Frontier Mercantile, blocking the breezeway to Adventureland that runs next to the Country Bear queue. The Bear Band host called his supervisor, who delivered her response with a steely eye: "Call Security. Tell them to bring bolt cutters."

And they did. One snip, and the Stroller Police were free to relocate the offender... right next to a Stinky the Stroller on the other side of the queue. (Yeah, we did that a lot.)

A few of us lingered to see who would claim it. A mom carrying a baby and dad lugging a toddler stopped short in front it, exchanged shocked glances to find their stroller had inexplicably moved. They wheeled around to find a cast member to chew out. They saw us; Mom's eyes narrowed.... Then they noticed the 6'-2" security guard standing next to us, staring back with the wry hint of a smile on his face.

Mom and Dad immediately cast their eyes down into the stroller, where they laid the baby. They pushed away, turning their heads to further avoid eye contact.

Yeah, we're the Stroller Police. Don't mess with us.

A *reader responds*:

When I went to the Magic Kingdom in September, we brought our daughter there for the first time. We went to the Mickey's Philharmagic show and parked her stroller in the large stroller parking lot that is off to the side of the 3D attraction. After the show, we walked back with the post-Philharmagic goofy smiles on our faces to collect our stroller, only to realize that it had been moved.

I scanned the sea of strollers to locate the one that had been moving my daughter around all day long. The stroller we had is a very popular stroller in an equally popular color - a fact that was made more apparent when we saw five of the same ones in the stroller lot. (Thank you, Babies R Us.) I had to go through the pockets of each one, violating so many rules of privacy just to find ours. Of course, ours was the last one I went through.

So we were leaving the area to move along when I noticed money in the pocket of the stroller's back. I asked my wife, "Hey did you put this in here?" She looked at me like I was crazy for suggesting she would leave money unattended. That is when I realized, oh wait, so this stroller isn't ours either. I then also realized, oh wait, this bottle of water I left in the stroller and have been drinking wasn't mine as well, because, as I just remembered, I hadn't bought a bottle of water yet that day!

So I ran back to the stroller parking, all the while fearing some disease that had infected me from drinking a stranger's bottle. Thoughts of H1N1 were circling my brain and I quickly imagined spending the remainder of the vacation curled up in a fetal position and cursing the name "Dasani"!

I quietly parked the stranger's stroller and casually walked away with the correct one. After that I ran straight to the bathroom and gargled with the hottest water I could stand. I was okay and remain completely H1N1 free to this day.

Another reader writes:

Someone had "abandoned" a stroller next to the ride I was operating. My ride was empty, so I was bored and watching a nearby squirrel... who jumped into the stroller!

I saw a bushy tail swishing around inside. A minute later, the squirrel slid out, dragging a chocolate chip cookie the size of my head. Mr. Squirrel chomped into the cookie just as the stroller's owners returned. Mr. Dad screamed, "That cookie was three dollars!" The squirrel hissed, and Mrs. Mom smiled and began taking pictures.

I went back to pretending I was working.

Waiting in line in the Magic Kingdom

At the start of my first summer working attractions in the Magic Kingdom, a weathered cast member who'd worked at the park since the day it opened told me this story. I assume it's theme park legend, but I wanted it to be true, because, like many apocryphal stories, it perfectly illustrates the way that theme park employees - and visitors - often feel about crowds in the parks.

Three cast members were "playing in the park" on their day off. For fun, they decided to queue up in front of the door to the riverboat crew's office, around the corner from the Hall of Presidents entrance, in Liberty Square. Sure enough, within a minute, a couple walked up to them.

"What are you in line for?" the man asked.

"I don't know, but we're first!" the leader of the three replied, while the others did their best to keep straight faces.

The man turned to his partner, shrugged, and joined the "line."

Within minutes on this busy summer day, two dozen others had joined the queue, which was now snaking toward the stockade that stands in front of the riverboat dock, about 20 yards away. When the line reached the riverboat's entrance, cutting off the path toward the

Haunted Mansion, the original three grinned at one another and the leader nodded. He turned to the first man who'd joined the queue.

"Darn it, it's almost time for our lunch reservations at the Diamond Horseshoe. Gotta go."

With that, the three walked over to the Horseshoe, suppressing laughs the whole way. As they passed the riverboat dock, the leader waved at the riverboat greeter, whom he knew, and said, "I don't know what's going on, but the crowd here looks like it's actually a line waiting for something in front of the crew office over there. You better check it out."

The three then ran for it, as the greeter walked over to the front of the crowd, wondering why a line would have formed in front of a unmarked (though well-themed) utility door.

"Excuse me, sir," he asked the man who'd first joined the queue, "but what do you think you are in line for?"

"I don't know," he replied.

"But I'm first!"

Quit thinking and just drive the raft

Before starting on the Tom Sawyer Island rafts that hot, humid June morning, my experience with watercraft was limited to canoeing while in Boy Scouts. I'd never sailed (which would have been far more relevant), so my trainer took me through the steps.

Unlash the stern. Push the bow away from the dock. Come around back and put the raft into forward gear. Straighten the tiller until the mast lines up with the Frontier Mercantile sign across the river. Wipe the sweat from your eyes.

When the raft comes up next to a certain shrub on what we called Duck Island, push the tiller all the way to the right to make the raft turn left. Hold the tiller there until the mast swings around to line up with the shack on the island dock. Then cut the throttle to neutral and swing the tiller the other way, all the way to the left. Wipe away more sweat.

Give the raft a blast in reverse to slow it down, then work the throttle between forward and reverse, as necessary, to ease it close to the dock. Put the tiller to the right when going forward and to the left when in reverse. Keep wiping that sweat.

Then lash the stern, put the throttle in forward, walk around to the front of the raft, tie off the bow and help guests off the boat. Smile through the sweat.

That was just the first half of the trip, mainland to island. There was another set of instructions for getting back.

Most of the time, I could "stick to the script" and get over and back without incident. But if I pushed off a little too hard when leaving the main dock, or started my turn at the wrong moment near Duck Island, I just didn't know how to adjust. I'd be stuck in the middle of the river for five minutes (or more!), blocking the canoes, keelboats and sometimes even the riverboat, as I rocked the throttle back and forth, swinging the tiller around, trying to find the magic combination that would lead me back to shore.

After a couple weeks, my supervisor had seen enough. It was time for retraining.

She sent me out the next morning, before the park opened, this time with a different trainer.

"So, how'd you learn to do this?" he asked.

"Well, I push off the bow, then line up the mast with the Frontier Mercantile sign."

"Oh, God, no."

He took the tiller and steered us to the middle of the river.

"Okay, Robert, drive the raft."

"Huh?"

"Just drive the raft. Take us wherever you want to go."

"I've always wanted to drive around the island," I said, looking away, a little embarrassed to admit I'd been thinking about driving the raft in a way that didn't match what I thought was the official training script.

"Let's go."

So we went, with me slowly nursing the raft around the Rivers of America.

"Speed up," my trainer said. "The faster you drive, the tighter you can make these turns."

For the next 10 minutes, we sailed around the island, with me taking the raft from riverbank to riverbank, wherever my trainer asked me to go. But he never told we what to aim for, or what on the raft to move - just where he wanted me to go. I felt the tiller and the throttle, how they worked together, and what combinations would move me where, and how quickly.

When we made it around, he asked me to dock on the island side. I swept the tiller to the side, and slid up next to the dock.

"Okay, let's head back."

I cast off, and with a smooth turn, brought the raft into the mainland dock.

"You're fine," he said, hopping off the raft and jogging into the office. "Don't worry about where the mast is pointing. Quit thinking about it.

"Just drive the raft."

I never missed the dock again.

Writing your own script

Most Disney World attractions jobs require some level of spieling - that is, speaking a script to guests. At minimum, you offer a few safety instructions as guests board a ride vehicle. At the other extreme, you're working a ride like Jungle Cruise, where your (hopefully) amusing spiel **is** the attraction.

By dumb luck, I was one of the few male cast members who worked more than a year in Magic Kingdom West attractions and never once pulled a shift in the Jungle. But that didn't stop me from telling silly jokes, too.

There was no script for spieling on Tom Sawyer Island. But I always enjoyed talking with (and performing for) the guests. So I made up some spiels, rather than stand in awkward silence while people looked at me. None of these were SOP (standard operating procedure, Disney-written spiels); I just made 'em up myself.

My favorite was a "safety" spiel:

"Good morning, everyone!" (Wait for response.) "Oh, come on, you can yell louder than that; I said good morning!" (Wait for response.) "My name is Robert and I'd like to welcome you to the Tom Sawyer Island rafts. Now our rafts are the only way over to Tom

Sawyer Island, which really is an island. It is completely surrounded by the Rivers of America.

"So just come on back to the raft dock where you arrived on the island when you want to return to Frontierland. Now, if you don't want to ride the raft back, though, there is one - and only one - other way back off the island.

"Everyone raise your right hand, over your heads, please." (I raised my hand, and waited for the crowd to do the same.) "Now put that down, and raise your left hand, over your head." (You have to envision us all raising and lowering our hands over our heads.) "Now, the right again, then the left, and the right... and if you want to add in a kicking motion, that'll help you get off the island a lot quicker, too.

"Or... you can just come on back to the dock and wait for the raft."

This spiel, in addition to waking everyone from their slumber before they visited what is, essentially, a playground, helped prevent the second most-frustrating question we got from guests: "Is there any way else back off the island?"

(The first most-frustrating question was, "Are these rafts on tracks?" Grrrr.....)

While driving the rafts, I also had a go-to line, which I delivered as I pushed the raft away from the mainland dock.

"If anything should go wrong during our trip, oxygen masks will drop from the compartments above your heads, and your seats may be used as a flotation device."

As anyone who has been on the ride might remember, the Tom Sawyer Island rafts have no roof and no seats. Still, every time I cracked this joke, some people looked up to find the masks, or down to find their seats. And their friends laughed at them for doing it.

A *reader responds:*

We were in Disney in December and got on a early ride of Jungle Cruise. The Skipper asked, were we all loaded? Of course we said, "Yes!" and his reply was, "Kind of early to be loaded, don't you think?" Of course, wanting to have a good time, I just could not resist replying, "It's 5 o'clock somewhere!"

Our skipper just laughed and said, "I see it's going to be one of those mornings already!" The rest of the cruise was one joke after another. A good time was had by all! Just goes to show that not just cast members can get in on the fun.

When nature calls...

Ultimately, you lived for the downtimes. You cherished any malfunction that broke the monotony, and introduced some variance into the shift.

My favorite little mis-hap? Well, you need to know that the Country Bear Jamboree show is totally mechanical, with hydraulics pushing, twisting, turning, raising, and lowering each of the bears. The "host," Henry, appears on three turntables, sharing the each space with another character, who rotates around from the other side of the turntable. For his first appearance in the show, Henry appears stage left, seated alone, wearing a green "Camp Grizzly" t-shirt and a pair of khaki shorts.

Henry bends forward at the waist when he laughs, controlled by a hydraulic line that runs up his core. And on this day, that line sprung a leak, spewing hydraulic fluid at a point just below the bear's waist.

Right through his khaki shorts.

That's right, Henry was wetting himself.

Being a good, show-conscious Disney cast member, I threw the switch to stop the show, apologized to the crowd and asked them to exit the theater. Not that anyone heard me over the laughter from the audience. It took me a good five minutes to break up the queue of people who'd gathered in front of Henry's turntable, to get their photo taken with the incontinent bear.

After I'd cleared the theater and we'd called maintenance to repair the show, there was the usual downtime paperwork. And neither my lead nor I could resist the temptation, when prompted to describe the reason for the downtime, to write:

"Henry peed his pants."

A reader responds:

I was working at Muppet Vision 3*D at the then-Disney MGM Studios. We had the same rotation, although we had a few extra positions dealing with 3D glasses. I came in to work one day, and was hanging out in Sweetums' greenroom (at the time we were permitted to hang out with them if they invited us). On the wall of the greenroom was a plastic tupperware container with one of the stuffed animal toys of Bean Bunny stuffed into it. The whole thing was duct taped to the wall with a note "In case of Emergency, Break Glass!" Puzzled, I asked why Bean was taped to the wall. One of the other cast members told me this story:

Like the bears, all of the animatronic figures in Muppets ran on hydraulic fluid. It seems that upon entering the theatre for the show, a guest had noticed that something had dripped on them. The cast member in the theatre position looked at the guest's clothing, and realized it was hydraulic fluid that had stained the shirt. Looking at the carpet, it was quickly determined that Bean Bunny, who appeared in the box seats over the entrance door, was the culprit. Being a good cast member, they had called the show down and emptied the theatre. Maintenance was called.

It took only five minutes, and maintenance cleared the show to reopen. That seemed like a short time, but if it was a minor leak, the cast could understand how it could be patched long enough to get through the day. They reopened. The show began, and progressed to the finale.

Now, for those who haven't seen the Muppet show at Disney, here's a brief rundown: Bean Bunny runs away because he isn't allowed to help with the show. He appears in the box as an Audio Animatronic (AA) after leaving the screen. Sweetums is dispatched by Kermit to help find Bean. He exits the screen and reappears in front of the screen bigger than life. Waving his flashlight around, he suddenly "finds" Bean in the box. "There he is!"

Except he wasn't there! In their infinite wisdom, the maintenance guys had simply removed the AA figure to take it back to their workshop, leaving nothing in its place. When Sweetums delivered his pre-recorded line, shining his flashlight up into the box, there was no bunny up there. Sweetums stomped off stage, the theatre cast member called the show 101, again, and emptied the theatre. In those days we took the "Show" part of our creed seriously, and a missing or damaged AA was cause to evacuate.

Maintenance was called again, and it was explained that we couldn't do the show without the bunny. They agreed to come back out to the attraction, and another five minutes later declared it operational.

Reluctantly, the cast loaded the theatre and started the show. Tentatively, Sweetums made his appearance. "Bunny?! Where are you Bunny?" The curtain to the box opened dramatically, and Sweetums shone his flashlight up into the darkness. "There he is!"

And there he was! Maintenance had gone over to the Stage One store, which sold Muppet related items, and had requisitioned a stuffed Bean Bunny toy. They had then stuck a ruler into Bean's, um, posterior, and designating one poor maintenance guy (low man on the totem pole I'm guessing) as puppeteer, having him lying on the floor of the box. When the curtain opened, Bean Bunny popped up out of the box, a rather unanimated stick puppet!

Sweetums threw a tantrum, storming off stage. The attraction was called 101 yet again until the real Bean Bunny could be repaired and returned. And the stick puppet was duct taped to the wall inside of someone's lunch container -- just in case!

Tempted by the smells of Adventureland

They'd warned me about the Treehouse.

Even before I started working in Adventureland attractions at Walt Disney World's Magic Kingdom, I'd known about the Swiss Family Treehouse. I'd enjoyed climbing through the treehouse when I was a kid - especially on those rare occasions, late at night, when there wasn't a crowd pushing like zombies from room to room. But based on the job description, I suspected that the treehouse wasn't going to be the most exciting place to work.

One cast member stood at the treehouse turnstiles, holding the line so that the crowd wouldn't overload the bridge over the old Swan Boat channel. When the crowd grew large, you'd opened the queue that snaked back and forth in a little hut behind the turnstiles. Mostly, though, you just stood out front and told folks, "No, this isn't the line for the Jungle Cruise. That's up ahead, on your left. Have a nice day."

So when another cast member took me aside to give me a warning before my first shift working the treehouse, I expected another lecture about boredom, about the importance of keeping a positive attitude, even as my brain began to rust from inactivity.

But that's not what she said.

"Try not to let the Egg Roll Wagon drive you crazy," she said.

The Egg Roll Wagon? That little food cart that set up next to the Treehouse queue? How would that drive me crazy? I couldn't remember a long line for it. Was there something strange about the foods person who worked it? Were they really bored, too? Were they going to drive me nuts with mindless chit-chat?

I walked past the wagon on my way to the treehouse. The foods person didn't even glance at me. The wagon looked perfectly normal. Why would anyone warn me about this?

And, then, I inhaled.

That smell. Ahhh, I understood. Standing here for two hours at a time, unable to purchase, much less eat, that which I was smelling would be the worst torture imaginable at Disney World.

If you've walked past the Egg Roll Wagon recently, you might not understand what I'm talking about. But I worked the treehouse years ago, back when the Adventureland Egg Roll Wagon sold the most aromatic delight ever offered in a theme park:

The Egg Roll Dog.

It was a hot dog, bathed in cheese, wrapped in a won ton skin and deep-fried, like an egg roll. Warming under the heat lamp, it broadcast the aroma of spicy beef, cheese and crispy goodness throughout the treehouse queue. It was bound to leave any perpetually hungry, 20-something cast member drooling.

Disney made more than a few dollars off its cast members with that cart. After my shift, I raced through the tunnels to change into my street clothes, just so I could race back to Adventureland and buy one of those Bad Boys.

Warm in my hands, I raised the egg roll to my mouth and bit into the crispy won ton wrapper, which shattered with my bite. Then the egg roll unleashed its flow of nuclear-hot liquid cheese, scorching my tongue so badly I had to let that precious first bite drop back into the napkin as I yelped in pain.

Which, of course, meant that I had to drop a few more bucks on a Dole Whip Float from the adjacent stand, to cool my blistered tongue. A few minutes later, my tongue had recovered and I finished the dog, washing it down with the pineapple juice from the float.

Fortunately, for my waistline and my bank account, I didn't work that many shifts that included stints at the treehouse. Instead, I spent many more days working safely away from the allure of the Egg Roll Wagon, pulling shifts in Frontierland.

Right next to the Turkey Leg Wagon.

Yes, we have no bananas in the Treehouse today

Have you ever taken the time to look closely at the lush plants growing throughout the Walt Disney World Resort? Standing next to the turnstiles while working at the Swiss Family Treehouse, I had a lot of time to notice the abundant flora in the Magic Kingdom's Adventureland.

I'm no horticulture expert. But I know a thing or two about food. So I did a double-take when I crossed the queue bridge to the treehouse steps on my pre-opening walk-through one morning.

"Are those... bananas?"

Sure enough, a bunch of very green, somewhat small bananas was growing in what had always looked to me like a nondescript bush next to the big fake Banyan tree trunk that supported the Robinsons' home.

I mentioned it to the cast member in charge of the area when I came back to the Tiki Room office for my break, lacking anything interesting to discuss after an hour watching disoriented guests plod through the treehouse queue, 90 percent of them thinking they were in line for the Jungle Cruise next door.

"You're kidding," he said, jumping from his chair. "I want to see."

As you can tell, it's an exciting life at the Tiki Room.

By the end of the day, word spread through the rest of the crew, and we'd concocted quite a plan for the bananas. We'd wait until just before they were ripe, then grab 'em. A day or two later, when they were soft and yellow, it'd be BananaFest behind the Tiki Room. Someone would bake some banana bread. We'd bring in ice cream for banana splits. We'd have all the bananas we could eat. I anticipated half the crew calling in sick from Potassium poisoning.

Our excitement backfired, though. The days in the Treehouse queue now passed even more slowly – if that could be possible. You say a watched pot never boils? Well, a watched banana takes its sweet time ripening, too.

A couple weeks later, we couldn't wait any longer. The decision was made - tomorrow morning, we're going in. Someone volunteered to bring a saw from home, to cut loose the bunch. Operation BananaFest was ready to commence.

(You're way ahead of me on this one, aren't you?)

I arrived for my shift the next morning to find a even more despondent Tiki and Treehouse crew waiting for me. The bananas were gone. Third-shift maintenance must have done the deed, someone said. Others had had their eyes on our bananas.

Our lead got into an argument with a maintenance lead, accusing them of swiping the bananas. The maintenance techs denied it. (We were all operating in a gray legal area here, since the bananas were Disney property, after all.) The bananas were gone, and we couldn't report it without looking like we'd been planning to steal them all along.

There was nothing we could do. So we all just tried putting it out of our mind. (Mind-numbing was a skill one needed to master working the treehouse queue.)

We'd done a pretty good job of it, too. Until the two mornings later, when we saw two maintenance techs responding to a pre-

41

opening call at the Jungle. As they walked by, we could see that they were eating... bananas.

Getting fired from the Haunted Mansion

We've talked about how important it is to smile if you want to work at a theme park. But smiling isn't always the way to advance in the theme park business.

My sister had been stuck working the Tiki Room for months. Every day, the same thing. Escort a small group of somewhat confused visitors into the dark, air-conditioned theater. Then start the show and "wake up" Jose, the animatronic bird, by tapping his perch with a stick. Then have a seat and wait... to start escorting the desperately bored visitors *out of* the dark, air-conditioned theater into the preferable, Tiki-bird-free Florida heat and sunshine.

Then repeat. Again, and again, and again.

So when my sister got word that she'd be cross-trained on the Haunted Mansion, she was ecstatic. After nearly a year of wearing the horrible polyester floral print of the Tiki room costume, she'd be donning the luxurious green polyester of the Haunted Mansion witches. Complete with the lace-trimmed "bat hat."

Training took several days, during which she was paired with an experienced Mansion hostess, who showed her how to operate the attraction. She learned how to time her steps as she walked the moving sidewalks at the loading and unloading areas, directing visitors into and out of their "Doom Buggy" ride vehicles. She learned how to slow and stop the walkway, to assist visitors in wheelchairs, and to assist anyone else who needed a little extra time to board and exit.

She learned the names of every scene in the ride, the characters that appeared throughout, and the history of the attraction, in case a visitor ever asked. (She had learned the same at the Tiki Room, but no one ever had asked about that show.)

She even learned something she'd never had to deal with at the Tiki Room - how to evacuate the ride. If something were to go wrong, and the Doom Buggies couldn't cycle around the building to drop off their passengers, Haunted Mansion hosts and hostesses would have to scatter throughout the ride, carefully helping visitors out of their vehicles and then walking them back through the show building to the ride's exit.

These were the most exciting days my sister ever had enjoyed working at the Magic Kingdom. Finally, something different! And at an attraction that people loved!

But despite all this training, Haunted Mansion hosts and hostesses aren't known for their ability to walk the moving sidewalks, or their evacuation prowess, or even their knowledge of Mansion trivia. Cast members who work the Haunted Mansion are best known for their roles at the beginning of the ride - their performances in the "stretch" room.

In Disney lingo, any moment a cast member spends out in the park is a moment "on stage." But working the stretch room really does feel like a performance. For a moment, all eyes are on you as you command the visitors into the "dead" center of the room. Here, cast members can get their goth on - the creepier the better. The best of the Mansion hosts and hostesses treat their stretch room visitors with an icy, almost haughty indifference.

As far as they're concerned, you're "dead" to them.

Unfortunately, my sister *did* care. Very much. She was so thrilled to be here, away from the Tiki Room and working one of the most popular theme park attractions at the world, that she could not bury her enthusiasm like it was the body of the Mansion's 999th ghost.

"Hello," she exclaimed as she bounded from the entry foyer, opening the attraction doors to her first group of waiting guests. "Welcome to the Haunted Mansion," she said, with her brightest, widest Disney casting-center smile.

Behind her, my sister's trainer rolled her eyes and stifled a groan.

After that group of guests exited the stretch room into the loading area, the trainer spoke to my sister in the now-empty stretch room.

"Um, next time," she said. "Could you, uh, try to be a little bit more, well, *witch*-y?"

"Sure," my sister said, hiding that she really didn't know what to do.

So with the next group of guests, my sister threw open the doors and proclaimed, in her deepest alto voice, "Welcome to the Haunted Mansion!"

For the rest of the morning, my sister kept trying to change the pitch of her voice and, eventually, the expression on her face. But it never lasted. She was just too happy. She couldn't stop smiling at the Haunted Mansion.

The next morning, as she bounded out of the tunnels and across Liberty Square toward the Mansion, the attraction's lead stopped her.

"Uh, I'm sorry," he told her. "It's not working out. We're sending you back to the Tiki Room. You're just too happy to work here."

Only that could finally wipe the smile from my sister's face at the Haunted Mansion.

The ultimate theme park weight-loss plan

Year after year, people list "losing weight" among their top new year's resolutions. For theme park fans who are looking to drop a few extra pounds, allow me introduce you to the most effective weight loss plan I've ever encountered:

The Tom Sawyer Island Plan

Step one: Drive (or fly) to the Walt Disney World Casting Center. You can use the west coast version of this plan by going to Disneyland's casting center, but you won't sweat off nearly as much weight working in Anaheim as you will working the summer in Orlando.

Step two: Apply for and get a job driving the Tom Sawyer Island rafts. Having freckles - like me - can be a big advantage here. Apparently, Disney casting reps really want to find the people most likely to fry in the sun.

Step three: Spend six to eight hours a day, standing up, driving shadeless rafts and walking up and down the paths on Tom Sawyer Island. Moving the raft tiller will work the upper body, providing your strength training, while walking the island gives you lower-body and cardio workouts.

Step four: Continue work into the summer, when Orlando's heat and humidity turn each shift into a six-to-eight-hour sauna, complementing your workout. (Bonus: If you can score an old-school, polyester double-knit Tom Sawyer Island costume, you'll sweat like a high school wrestler in a rubber suit, trying to make weight.)

Step five: Take your fitness to the next level by extending to work the roll-out crew for Parade Audience Control. Clipping parade route ropes together provides a high-tension resistance workout, while rolling the parade rope from a 40-lb. spool strapped to your chest is the ultimate in Disney attractions weight training.

(Advanced students who find that the Tom Sawyer Island Plan no longer delivers desired results may choose at this time to transfer to entertainment and don a full-body character suit. Ideally one with a ginormous, heavy head. This not only doubles the sauna effect, but also develops your balance and ESP, as you attempt to identify little kids who'll pull your tail before they actually do.)

After just three months on this plan, you'll often find yourself in the Disney cast cafeteria, scarfing down a 5,000-calorie basket of nachos... while still losing weight.

Some folks might try to sell you on the Haunted Mansion Plan, with its miles and miles of walking the load and unload belts. While that plan is a great choice for people who want a long-distance cardio workout, the Mansion's indoor setting will rob you of the outdoor sauna effect. In addition, you won't get the same upper body work as you will wrestling the Tom Sawyer Island rafts.

Unfortunately, Disney has discontinued its sadistic "Mike Fink Keelboats Plan," which provided all the benefits of the Tom Sawyer Island Plan, while forcing you to balance on a rickety keelboat while also spieling - doubling the cardio work and forcing you into in a yoga-like level of breath control.

See your Disney casting rep to sign up today!

The lightning capital of America

Lightning pummels Central Florida. The stretch from Tampa to Orlando is America's Lightning Capital, with more than 90 thunderstorms a year, on average, and more than 15 strikes per square kilometer. Tampa named its pro hockey team after it. And it shuts down many theme park attractions most days during the summer.

I've been nearly hit by lightning twice in my life, and both incidents happened in Central Florida. The most recent was on a flight from Orlando to Atlanta, where the plane was hit not too long after takeoff. It was a 7 a.m. flight, and I was dozing – until a loud crack and blinding flash brought me to full consciousness. All I remember seeing was the red of my eyelids, which squeezed shut with the flash.

The first incident happened years ago, when I was working a shift on Tom Sawyer Island. Fortunately, I had docked my raft before the rain hit. (That wasn't always the case, as well see later.) So I was waiting with the guests who'd sought shelter in the mainland waiting area.

The roof over the wait area slopes down, also covering a bit of the raft dock. That's where I waited, on the east side of the dock, toward what we called Duck Island. Duck Island was a small patch of land near the riverbank, barely large enough for a couple trees. But it was inconveniently located - we had to push the bow of the raft away from the mainland dock every time we cast off, in order to avoid running aground on it. And while the island was small, the trees on it were not. I worked at Tom Sawyer Island before Disney built Splash Mountain, and at the time, the trees of Duck Island were the tallest point between the Pecos Bill restaurant and Big Thunder Mountain Railroad.

I was chatting with another cast member and a few guests who were waiting under the shelter. For some reason, I turned toward Duck Island, and felt every hair on my arms rise. Sportscasters abuse the phrase "there's electricity in the air," but if you've ever literally felt that, the memory of that sensation never will leave you.

My brain had no time to process what was happening before the crushing blast. It's funny, but looking back upon the strike, I felt like I'd anticipated it. That's because the brain sends out the command to "Get down: NOW!" before it passes along to your consciousness the news of the incoming crack and flash which elicited that command.

I found myself curled up in a ball under the queue rail on the raft dock, before I knew what had almost hit me.

A charcoal smell hit my nose, forcing open my eyes. The guests I'd been chatting with were on their knees, and the ones behind them stood, faces frozen, staring toward Duck Island. A child cried. I looked toward the island, and saw a tree's arm, severed to the ground, bridging the water between the island and the dock's exit pathway. The cooling rain returned. No one was hurt, and nothing was damaged.

Save the tree, of course, whose fallen branches maintenance crews soon cleared.

In addition to the lightning, the afternoon thunderstorms bring rain. Immense amounts of rain. And those thunderstorms happen faster than most visitors can imagine.

Another summer afternoon, I was loading a raft for a trip back from the island to the mainland. The clouds gathered quickly that day, darkening the sky over the Splash Mountain construction site to a roiling black. Yet the skies over the island remained sunny. One father squinted as he looked up into the sky and asked me, with a kidding tone, "How long do you think we'll have until that rain hits?"

"If you are lucky," I replied as I cast off and put the raft into gear, "we'll make it to the other side of the river first."

He laughed at what he thought was my joke. I laughed at him for thinking that.

Halfway across the river, I announced to the raft, in my loudest stage voice, "Please no open umbrellas on the raft. Wait until we dock before opening umbrellas."

Several people turned to look at me, with puzzled expressions. The sky was sunny, why are you talking about....

Then the rain hit. A torrential, Old Testament rain. One for which no rain jacket or umbrella provides any protection. The type of rain that leaves your underwear soaked for the remainder the day.

To their credit, my raft guests heeded my warning and did not open their umbrellas. (You don't want to get poked in the head with one when our free-floating raft bumps the dock.) I don't know whether they respected my authority or simply understood, as I did, that umbrellas were of no use against this vertical flood.

I docked my raft, nodded at my supervisor, then headed down to the costume department for a fresh, dry costume – and a change of underwear (which I always kept in my locker). You could tell the rookies among Disney cast members. Those were the ones who, after a soaking rainstorm like this, were wearing dry replacement costumes, through which their dripping underwear was soaking.

A reader responds:

I worked at Kali River Rapids. We stayed open during the rain, but not during thunderstorms.

At the beginning of the queue, there is an umbrella that holds water really, really well when it rains. So when already rain-soaked guests came by to line up for the ride, I would ask them "Are you ready to get soaked?" They usually gave an enthusiastic answer. I would say, "Great! 'Cause it starts now!" at which point I would tip the umbrella over, causing all the water that was trapped to splash all over the guests. We'd all have a good laugh, and the guests were having a good time.

But not every time.

One lady, who was already completely drenched, with a smile on her face, was starting to line up. So I went through my spiel:

Me: "Are you ready to Tackle the Kali??"

Lady: "Oh yeah!"

Me: "Awesome! Here's a preview!"

Except this time, when I tipped the umbrella, the lady stopped, turned to me with the meanest look that I have ever seen, pointed her finger at me and yelled at the top of her lungs:

"WHAT THE F#&* WAS THAT ALL ABOUT?"

I stopped dead in my tracks. Saying I had a deer-in-headlights look would be an understatement.

She continued: "I did NOT line up for this ride to get wet!"

Confused, I responded, "But ma'am this is Kali River Rapids...you ARE gonna get wet."

She didn't skip a beat, "What are you talking about, this is the Everest roller coaster ride. Are you stupid?"

At this point, I'm started to get pretty angry. But, keeping my Disney cool, I showed her a map and pointed her to Everest (which was closed). At this point, she started mumbling something about Jesus and lightning, with a few cuss words thrown in there.

Another reader replies:

I can't remember the year, but I was working at the Pocahontas show at what was then Disney-MGM Studios. (Yes, there used to be a Pocahontas show there). People queued for at least 45 minutes for that show, always, so we were very conscientious about not canceling it unless we really had to. The show was about to start, and the sky was rapidly turning to midnight black. I was in operations, assisting guests with finding seats, and my position for the show was right in front of the stage. We had confirmed with the stage manager that he did, in fact, want to go ahead and do the whole show, since we were really nervous about the obviously impending storm that was moving very quickly toward us. The stage manager assured us silly operations folks that they had plenty of time to finish the show before the storm hit.

At that time, the backlot theater was still a somewhat temporary structure. Benches weren't bolted down, and the "roof" was a canopy structure on metal supports. Guests sat on metal benches and a metal riser stand, so it was imperative that we get them out of the theatre in cases of lightning. The storm appeared to be very violent, and we were extremely concerned that we would have to evacuate in the middle of the show. We had no idea!

Pocahontas and John Smith were just about to launch into "Colors of the Wind" when the colors of the wind changed from lovely blue to ugly grey and black, immediately! The wind picked up and the type of rain that blows completely sideways, if not upside down, began pouring from the sky like someone had dumped one of the water-tank effects on us. The wind was howling so loudly that no one could hear anything over it. The show lights turned off, the cast basically ran off stage, and we were stuck with guests who were not going to run out into the rain if you paid them. There was limited cover in the theater, they were determined to stay under it.

A couple of us looked up at the canopy at about this time, and our hearts collectively stopped in mid-beat. The metal supports were actually buckling under the weight of water that was rapidly filling the canopy! Several small tears were forming in it, dripping into the theatre. The only question was whether the canopy would split and dump a ton of water on us, or whether the supports would buckle and drop the whole canopy on us first.

We collectively sprang into action. Attractions cast members on either side of the stage began literally pushing guests out into the rain, shouting at the top of our lungs that they had to get to safer cover. Those on my side ran to the Muppets theater, which (ironically) had received a lightning strike just before the rain had started and had evacuated, leaving the building empty. We were pushing the guests out toward the Muppets cast, who for their part were welcoming them into the building, wrapping the wetter of them in Muppet costume lab coats and throwing towels to them. The guests, seeming to understand our urgency, were cooperative and ran for shelter at our command.

The way that theater was set up, guests with disabilities sat in the front row. The house was raked, sloping down toward the stage to offer a better view for those in the back. The tissue paper leaves that we dumped on the audience during "Colors of the Wind" tended to block the drains. As we were pushing guests out, we noted that the front of the theatre was filling up with water, and the guests in wheelchairs were now up to their knees in it! We ran down to the front, and each of us grabbed a guest in a wheelchair, pushing the chairs up to higher ground. Many of our guests were elderly couples, and many of their companions couldn't get the chairs up the slope fast enough. We all took off our rain gear, draping it over those guests in wheelchairs before pushing them out into the rain. Companions and other guests took over, pushing those soggy people to the safety of the Muppet building. By now, the water was nearly up to the level of the stage, and those who could walk had abandoned their wheelchairs and made a run for it.

Finally, we had all the guests out. We were all drenched, having given up our rain gear (which really hadn't done us much good anyway, considering the violence of the storm). The rain was still coming down sideways, and more breaches in the canopy were showing. The stage manager hollered for us to come up on stage. He turned on all the stage lights so we could warm up and dry off a little.

I remember sitting there, on a tree stump on stage, watching the rain. What I remember most, though, is the sight of one lone wheelchair, floating by the front row, which by now was nearly under water.

From that point on, we cancelled shows whenever the weather threatened.

One more reader story:

I work at the Tower of Terror, and we really don't get many weather-related stories. But this one ranks at the top of my all time "people don't think" stories!

When it rains, a good portion of guests put on rain ponchos. At the Tower, we ask guest to take off their ponchos and put them away, so that they don't go flying when the ride vehicles drop.

Well, once while working as a supervisor, I saw a guest get into an elevator with a yellow rain poncho. I stopped the cast member who was loading the elevator.

He thought about it, looked into the elevator and he said he didn't know what was wrong. I told him that somebody was wearing a poncho, which is not allowed. I went over to the elevator and asked the guest to take off their poncho. And lo-and-behold: there, underneath the poncho, was a five-month-old baby!

I couldn't believe what I was seeing. The other cast member was in disbelief, and even the other guest were in awe. I called up the manager and told him what happened. The manager warned the guest not to take the baby on other rides where there is a height restriction.

After this happened, I noticed that the rain ponchos soon changed from yellow to the clear-colored ponchos you see today.

Someone always knows the score

The San Francisco Giants were playing the Chicago Cubs in the National League Championship Series, for the right to go on to the World Series. As a recent Northwestern graduate, I was pulling for the Cubs, but it was a family of Giants fans who walked up to the turnstiles at Pirates of the Caribbean that day.

Now, I'm going to take a moment to remind our younger readers about ancient history. Back in 1989, the World Wide Web was yet to become a glimmer in Tim Berners-Lee's eye. Cell phones were car phones - big, bulky and used pretty much only by real estate agents, doctors, and lawyers. If you wanted to know a sports score, you either found a television set and waited for an update or, if you were a degenerate gambler, you found a pay phone that would let you make a call to a "976" line and fed it coins until the recorded message gave the score you wanted.

The Giants fans in my queue would have liked to watch the game that day, but they'd planned their Walt Disney World visit for months. They hadn't expected the Giants to make it this far - heck, history had taught them that October belonged to other fans' teams. So they skipped the game for their theme park vacation.

But they still wished to know the score. There aren't any television sets in the Magic Kingdom, but I suppose they guessed there were some in break rooms around the park. So they took a chance and asked me.

"Hey, you wouldn't happen to know the score to the Giants-Cubs game, would you?"

I was about to say, "No," when I remembered my Disney University training: Disney cast members never respond that they don't the answer to a question. They find out.

But how was I going to find out the score to a baseball playoff game, standing at the entrance to Pirates of the Caribbean?

Like any good corporate employee, I decided to kick this question up the ladder. I called park control.

Normally, front-line cast members don't call park control unless they are reporting that an attraction has shut down unexpectedly. But, hey, Disney had told me I couldn't say no, so someone at Disney owed me an answer.

"Hello, this is Robert at Pirates of the Caribbean. This is going to sound a bit unusual, but I have a guest here who'd like to know the score of the Giants-Cubs game and I don't want to tell him that I don't have an answer. Do you know where I can get that score for him?"

To this day, I am as proud of the way I phrased that question as I am of anything else I've ever written. I completely inoculated myself and put the park control operator in a position where he couldn't tell me to buzz off. A guest had a question, and Disney policy was that he gets his answer.

"Ummmm... hold on a second."

I could tell that the park control operator was trying to think of a place where he could kick this question, too. A minute passed, but I wasn't hanging up the phone. While I waited, I chatted up the Giants fans, learning about how they'd planned their trip and admitting to them that as a Northwestern grad, I was rooting for the Cubs. The dad was surprised to hear that I was from Northwestern, and told me about a co-worker who'd gone to NU, too.

Finally, the operator got back on the line. Whatever he'd done to find an answer, it had worked.

"The Giants won: 6-4."

I thanked the operator, then told the family. They were ecstatic. The dad shook my hand and thanked me, as the son pumped the air with his fist and leapt down the entrance hall.

Of course, today you'd probably just hop on your cell phone to answer a question like that. But should them new-fangled Interwebs ever fail to deliver, it's nice to remember that whenever you have a question at Walt Disney World, someone always knows the score.

When I didn't keep my hands and arms inside the boat at all times

I worked full-time at Disney for a year between college and graduate school, and during that time, Disney promoted me to an attractions "lead," which was Disney's lowest level of management. You were paid by the hour, just like the regular workers, but you were in charge of those other cast members at your specific attraction during your shift.

One of a lead's duties was to check the "show quality" of the attraction at the start of your shift. The opening lead would ride through (or walk through) the attraction, to see if all the major animation elements were working properly and that the show scenery was in good condition.

On busy rides such as Pirates of the Caribbean, the lead would take a ride during the middle of the day as well, often in response to a specific guest complaint about something not working on the ride. That's how I came to be sitting alone in the back row of a Pirates boat one summer afternoon. Someone had said that poor, bald Carlos wasn't taking his little swim at the end of his rope in the "dunking" scene, so I rode through to check him out.

Once on board, I had to ride the full 10 minutes all the way around to the end of the ride, like everyone else. But even that ride-through would take less time than walking all the way through the building to watch Carlos from the opposite flume bank.

Carlos was fine, and I counted through my mental checklist as I floated through the rest of the ride: Auctioneer, turntables (the pirates chasing the women, plus the one woman chasing a pirate), the singing trio, the burning city. Check, check, check and check.

Halfway through the burning city, our boat bumped into the line of stalled boats, backed up from the end of the ride. "That's not good," I thought to myself, wondering if a wheelchair party was taking extra time exiting several boats in front me, slowing the unload line.

Slow is one thing. Stopped another. After a minute, we hadn't budged, and the "rascals and scoundrels and really bad eggs" endlessly pillaging the village were beginning to rattle my nerves.

Then... the music stopped. Really not good. I knew what was coming next: the spiel.

"Ahoy there, mateys. Please remain seated. Your voyage will resume in a few moments."

Great. My ride just went down... with me on it.

I had no way to talk to the cast members in the ride's control tower – this was before cell phones, back when only supervisors and parade leads in Walt Disney World Attractions carried two-way radios. There were no other trained leads in the rotation – just me. I needed to get back into tower, and quickly.

Unfortunately, I was stuck in the burning city, a scene in the ride with no exit point - no easy place to hop out of the boat and walk backstage to the tower. So I did something that you're never, ever supposed to do.

I reached over the side of the boat, grabbed the metal flume wall under the water and began pulling my boat back toward the singing trio and the nearest exit point.

By this time, several more boats had backed up behind mine. So I as pulled back my boat, I pushed the weight of those boats, as well. This made it a two-handed task. Hold with one hand, then reach over with the other and pull. Repeat. Meanwhile, everyone around me wondered what the heck this guy in a pirate suit was doing, hanging half-way out of the back of a boat and dunking his hands underwater.

Ignoring the confused looks, I backed the boat close enough to the bridge before the burning city scene, where I could jump off. That point is where we add extra boats to the ride from the hidden storage area, so there's a intercom phone tucked behind some of the fake trees.

As I jumped off, I turned back toward the folks in the boats and asked them to remain seated, promising that someone would be with them very soon. I grabbed the phone, called up to tower, and let the operator know I was on my way.

A belt had failed at unload station, keeping the boats from moving past that point. Sure enough, we had to evacuate. With the house lights on and the ride pumps off, we soon had other "pirates" in the water, pushing boats to the various unload points. Within 10 minutes, the attraction was clear and maintenance was working to repair the belt.

But that remains the one and only time I ever had to evacuate *myself* from Pirates of the Caribbean.

Why you have to be 40 inches tall to ride Disney's Big Thunder Mountain

You can't possibly think of a new way to get around a roller coaster's height requirement that theme park employees haven't seen before.

Lifts in the shoes? Seen it.

Spiked up hair? Not gonna get ya through.

Standing on your tippie toes? Um, feet flat on the ground, please.

Begging, pleading, crying? Actually, we are the ones trying to help your child here.

That's because, as theme park employees working a roller coaster, we know what can happen when a too-short child rides a coaster.

Now, I'll start with a confession. In normal operation, we could take an infant on Walt Disney World's Big Thunder Mountain Railroad and no harm would come to the baby. I worked with cast members who could eat a bowl of cereal while riding a test train on Thunder in the morning and not spill a drop of milk. They clearly knew the ride well enough to hold a baby securely throughout. I don't doubt that some Disney fans could do the same.

But theme parks don't establish height requirements based on a ride's normal operation. They put requirements in place to protect riders in case something goes wrong on the ride.

By that, I don't mean a mechanical breakdown. I mean that something happens, usually because of a guest's actions, which disrupts the normal flow of operation on the ride. What happens when a child starts crying in a train, which prevents us from dispatching it from the loading station?

With no room in the station, the train behind on the track has no place to go. So it stops out on the course, on the final block brake. With a train on that brake, the train behind it has to stop on the third lift. And so on.

Those "cascade" stops happen in orderly manner, and probably wouldn't make an experienced rider spill his milk (or drop a child). But what happens when a guest panics, and tries to jump out of a train while it's on a lift? It's happened, and I've seen it.

In cases like that, the operator in the coaster's control tower does a "power disconnect," shutting down power to the entire track. Any train on a lift will stop immediately. But trains that have crested their lifts will continue running, propelled simply by the free fall of gravity along the track.

To keep those trains from running into one that might be stuck on the next lift, ride designers have installed what's called a "safety brake" in front of each lift. And *that* is what you do not want to hit if you are shorter than 40 inches tall, or pregnant, or have a back, neck or heart condition. A safety brake can take a train running nearly 30 miles per hour to stopped in about eight feet. It's a hard, hard stop.

No one ever wanted to be the one assigned to go check on the guests who'd been stopped in a safety brake after the ride shut down with trains on the track. Only the most experienced Thunder operators were assigned that task, and even though I worked that location for a year, I never had enough seniority to draw that thankless assignment. (I was always sent to people stuck on a lift, instead.) But I heard reports from those who did about the sore, shocked and sometimes angry guests who had to endure the misfortune of hitting the safety brakes.

Still, I never knew anyone to be hurt from hitting a safety brake, as unpleasant as that experience must have been. To me, that's testimony to the effectiveness of Disney's boarding restrictions.

So next time a cast member, team member or theme park employee stops a too-short child from getting on a ride, don't make the cast member the bad guy. The more you know about how roller coasters work, the more you might appreciate the important work that the people at the front of the queue do everyday.

A reader responds:

Splash Mountain is the same way. On a normal ride, there's absolutely no reason you couldn't take a baby on it. However, if there happens to be an Emergency Stop while a log is going down the big drop, a brake at the bottom will activate and bring the log to a stop almost instantly. It doesn't happen often, as the timing has to be just right, but I've watched it on the monitors in tower. You do not want to have a baby in your arms or a child on your lap if you happen to be in the log that gets caught.

I used to be really bothered by parents who would argue that their children should be allowed to go on the ride, even though they were too short. A woman once told me that she was a lawyer and would write a waiver to allow her kid to go. I thought it was terrible that, as a 19-year-old college student, I was more concerned for the safety of these kids than their parents were.

The most difficult question, ever

What's the single most difficult thing a theme park cast member is ever called upon to do?

Move a crowd of people off the street and behind a Magic Kingdom parade barrier? Maybe, but with a strong voice and a stronger attitude, that's really no big deal.

Calm a crying child before he stops the line at load? Also tricky, but a warm smile and kneeling down to a child's eye level can do wonderful things.

Wiping up a "protein spill" after said child finishes that ride? Disgusting, but less so once one discovers that invaluable substance, "Vo-Ban" (the stuff you sprinkle over fresh upchuck to make it stink less.)

No, this single most difficult thing a theme park employee has to do is...

Ask a woman if she is pregnant.

If she says 'yes,' hey, not only have you done your job well, but maybe you also just prevented a horrible incident that could have compromised her pregnancy.

But if she says 'no'... hell hath no fury like a woman mistaken for a pregnant one.

I'll always remember one soul-destroying exchange I witnessed at Walt Disney World's Big Thunder Mountain load platform:

"Excuse me, ma'am, but are you pregnant?"

"PREGNANT? No! What are you saying, do I look FAT?"

"Um," (awkward pause) "actually, I was saying that I thought you looked, maybe, pregnant."

At this moment, every other operator on the platform looked away, trying to shrink behind the nearest stanchion, or, ideally, into a hole in the floor.

"I AM NOT PREGNANT! Oh my God," the young woman then buried her head into her friend's chest and sobbed. "They think I look fat. Let's get out of here!"

Then they crossed over the train and out the station, as the poor cast member who asked her the question looked like he'd just as soon throw himself in front of said train.

Bad times, all around.

Still, you've got to ask. The consequence of letting an expectant mother on some rides can be horrific. You remember that "safety brake" that stops a fast-moving coaster in eight feet? You do not want a pregnant belly anywhere near a lap bar when a roller coaster hits that safety brake.

I never, ever wanted to be that cast member, who felt just as humiliated asking the question as that poor woman felt having to answer it. Which is why I felt the weight of the world lift from me one day as I discovered an impromptu solution.

A maybe-pregnant, maybe-not young woman was walking down the platform at load. As she walked closer, and the moment of truth approached, I turned to the pair of teenage boys in front of me and asked, in a booming voice with a huge smile on my face...

"Are you pregnant?"

They looked at me like I was nuts. But I didn't wait for an answer. I then asked the elderly ladies behind them the same question.

"Are you pregnant?"

She just laughed. To the burly biker dudes behind them,

"Are you pregnant?"

They laughed, too, as the woman-in-question finally approached, laughing along with the rest of the platform.

"No," she said.

Soul-crushing moment averted!

I kept asking down the line for that entire train, just for appearances. That became my Standard Operating Procedure for every potential pregnancy then on: ask *everyone* around the woman in question if they were pregnant, so that the woman would not feel singled out.

Many times, I saw a panicked look on the woman's face as I approached, and I knew that she would be answering 'yes.' When that happened, I stopped the schtick, changed to an earnest expression of concern and explained, "Oh, gosh, I'm sorry, ma'am, but we can't allow expectant mothers to ride. Here, please come stand right over here," as I would help her across the train to the unload side and changed my expression to a wide smile, "and you can wait for your group while they ride."

Never failed, and no one ever complained.

The Old Man and the Caribbean Sea

"Sorry for the hold-up, folks. Seems to be a slow-moving train up ahead. You just remain seated, and we'll be right with ya."

The "Old Man" was up, which meant we were down at Big Thunder Mountain Railroad. I'd been trained at Thunder only a couple weeks earlier, but had already learned about the Old Man - the pre-recorded spiel of a supposed prospector that played automatically whenever the roller coaster's computer system shut down the ride.

A little kid on the main side station had been crying, so the crew held the train. Disney rules prohibit dispatching a ride vehicle with a crying child: The child has to either stop crying, or get off the ride. We would allow families to wait on the unload platform as long as necessary until their child stopped bawling, then reseat them on the next train. But no train was going anywhere with a crying kid on it.

Unfortunately for everyone in line, if the family of the crying kid didn't accept the, uh, invitation to wait to the side, that train could not leave. And if one train didn't leave on time, that meant there was no room in the station for the train behind it on the track, outside the station. (Thunder has two stations, with up to five trains on the track.) The Old Man was getting up, and the ride was going down.

Coming back up from a "cascade stop" such as this was relatively simple. You just get everyone off the train in the station, then send it back into the storage area. Then you bring in the next train off the track, unload its guests, and then send it back into storage. You keep doing that until all the trains are either in storage or in a station. Then you bring the trains back onto the circuit, one at a time, until you're running the three, four or five trains you need - depending upon the size of the crowd in the park.

The cast member who was working Thunder's control tower when the Old Man woke up was the one to oversee the restart. On that day, the guy in the tower just happened to be a guy who, like me, had been working several months at Pirates of the Caribbean and just recently cross-trained on Thunder. This was his first-ever downtime on the roller coaster.

The ride's lead hurried up to the tower to assist. Had a more experienced cast member been working in the tower, the lead would have just stood by and chatted with cast members and guests. Today, the lead stood closer, watching as the rookie slowly worked his way through the procedures.

When the trains stop on the lifts throughout the ride, we turned on the ride's work lights and sent operators to each lift, first to calm the riders, then to restart the lifts. We always worked our way backwards, starting one lift at a time, so that no one would have a train rushing by him or her while out on the track. Because there were operators on the track, the tower operator had to announce over the loudspeakers as each section of track restarted.

And he did. Oh boy, did he!

"Attention on Pirates of the Caribbean. Block zone four is restarting."

Knowing the rookie was fresh over from Pirates, several of the Thunder vets started to giggle, then caught themselves. I, a Thunder newbie like the rookie, simply thought, "There but for the grace of the Old Man, go I" and kept my mouth shut.

"Attention on Pirates of the Caribbean. 'C' lift is restarting."

At that point, no one on the load platform could contain themselves. The dispatcher on my side of the station actually doubled over in laughter. Even guests in the crowd turned to one another, asking, "Did he just say what I thought he did?"

"Attention on Pirates of the Caribbean. 'B' lift is restarting."

The crowd on the load platform started to laugh. The dispatcher on my side composed himself enough to start singing "Yo Ho, Yo Ho, A Pirate's Life for Me." Many in the crowd joined in.

Already overwhelmed by his first solo restart of the ride, and now utterly perplexed by the reaction on the platform, the rookie leaned over the mic to announce the next lift restart.

"Attention on Pi-"

Recognition dawned scarlet on his face. He eyes grew with terror, then squeezed shut. The lead was about to draw blood, she was biting her hand so hard to keep from laughing.

"Uh, attention on Big Thunder Mountain, 'A' lift is restarting," the rookie croaked.

The Thunder cast members erupted in applause. The dispatcher who'd been conducting the crowd stood tall and pointed toward tower: "That's right! Y'all's on THUNDER MOUNTAIN now!"

The rookie drank free that night.

A *reader asks:*

I thought the more interesting part of the story was how a ride breaks down and powers back up. I also never knew that Disney will not let a crying child on a ride. Is it because it would ruin the magic for the other guests or is there some other reason?

Another reader responds:

It's actually more a safety concern than aesthetics. At least it was on Rock 'n' Roller Coaster. If a child is crying in the station, they aren't wanting to ride. They're scared. They might panic mid-ride and try to squirm out of safety restraints, or hurt themselves in their panic. The rule about not letting crying children ride is left to the discretion of the cast members. If the child is just sniffling, but seems ready to ride, we dispatch away. If the child is crying and obviously doesn't want to go, we make the parents remove him. Unlike Thunder though, we didn't have a problem if someone took awhile deciding. We could back up a bit and not go down.

Convincing parents that we had the safety of their kids in mind wasn't always easy, though. We heard, "I paid all this money for you to ride rides, and damn it, you're going to ride them!" more than once.

I had one really terrific father one time though. He got on the ride with the kid, who then panicked. We asked him to step aside, and he did, choosing to stand in the area just on the platform side of the exit hallway. My position was on the platform, and my location to stand between trains was right on the other side of the safety gate from where the father and his son were standing. Father talked to the kid, finding out exactly what he was afraid of. I answered some questions, and confirmed a lot of what the father was saying. He didn't lie to the kid. We heard that a lot: "It's not scary," or "You don't go upside down," (you do) or "It's not really a roller coaster" - terrific parenting, telling lies to your kid to get them to go on a coaster. He didn't negate or berate the kid's fears. He talked to him and encouraged him. Doggone it if that kid didn't tug on my sleeve about five minutes later asking if it was too late to ride. I told him of course it wasn't, and put him on the next train. He looked petrified, but determined. I was bumped onto the next position while he was in the launch area and was sent to the ride's exit platform. I was there when he arrived in the station. He had a HUGE grin on his face. "Can I ride again?" he immediately asked his Dad. His father couldn't have looked prouder if he'd tried! I put them both back through the re-ride hallway to do it again. Anyone who's that brave deserves another run!

Another reader replies:

Working at Kali River Rapids, the same rule applies: if a kid is crying, they cannot leave the loading area. Like at Thunder, we can bring them to the center of the loading turntable to regain their composure, or they could choose not to ride, but we couldn't let them off until the kid stops crying. Well, we had a family who wouldn't leave, like in Robert's story. The parents were stubborn and wouldn't leave until they rode the ride. The kid, however, wasn't having any of it. He was bawling so hard, he sounded like he was being tortured. He was trying to get his seat belt off, he wouldn't sit down, and he had that "Get me out of here!" look on his face. While another cast member, a coordinator, a manager and I were trying to calm the kid down and get him off the ride, the parent was yelling at us to turn the ride back on.

At this point, everybody in the other rafts and in queue started to pick up on what was going on. I had to explain to everybody what was going on, and what we had to do. Everybody understood, but they were growing impatient with the parents. About half way up the ramp that comes down to the turntable, there were a group of 5 or 6 frat boys. I could see they were scheming something. I turned around to head back to the turntable, and I heard a chant starting behind me:

"HEY! HEY! WHAT DO YOU SAY? GET YOUR KID OFF SO WE CAN RIDE TODAY!"

What do you know, it was the frat boys. Everybody started to giggle, and even some started to join in. The coordinator went over to shush them, while at the same time, the family was getting out of the raft. The entire queue starts to applaud. At this point, I caught a look at the father in the group...and this is when my heart jumped into my throat. To explain what he looked like, some would say Lou Ferrigno, some would say Hulk Hogan without the mustache, I would say all of the above...and he wasn't a happy camper. The mom held the child, yelling at him while they were walking off the turntable, with the father behind. As he was leaving, the dad and one of the frat boys met eyes...oh boy...

Now I have never seen a fist fight while working at Disney World, but this was the closest I have ever seen one. The frat boy said something, and the dad grabbed the frat boy by the collar and said something like, "Stay out of my sight," and something about ripping genitals, I'm not really sure, I wasn't that close. At this point, the frat boys were trying to save their buddy and the manager was grabbing Lou Hogan away from everybody else. Everybody on the turntable, guests and cast alike, were trying to see what was going to happen.

Ahhh... there's nothing like working at "the happiest place on Earth."

A very unwanted souvenir

How'd you like a job where you do nothing but stand in front of a closed theme park ride all day?

That happens when theme park attractions go down for their regular refurbishments. When I worked at Walt Disney World's Magic Kingdom, the employees who typically worked a closed attraction would be reassigned to other attractions in the same area. (Almost everyone was trained on multiple attractions.) But one person was still assigned as a "greeter" at the closed attraction, and his job was simply to confirm to guests that, yes indeed, that attraction was closed.

The greeter was supposed to be friendly, suggest other things to do, and answer questions about the park. So the gig wasn't as boring as it might seem, especially for cast members, like me, who enjoyed talking with guests.

But some locations offered more chance to talk with folks than others. When I worked at Disney World, the park drained the Rivers of America for its regular cleaning and repair, closing Tom Sawyer Island, the riverboat and canoes. Disney also was building a pedestrian bridge across a corner of the river, to accommodate Splash Mountain, which was then under construction.

As a result, a construction wall lined the entire perimeter of the River, as well as another construction wall on the other side of the pathway, where Splash Mountain was going up. This created a narrow, walled pathway heading to up Thunder Mountain, through which everyone had to pass when going to and coming from the roller coaster's entrance and exit.

This bottleneck was also where they stuck the poor cast member from Tom Sawyer Island. Usually when an attraction is down for rehab, you can still tell that the ride is there: The front door is just closed and the queue is blocked. But with construction walls blocking all views of the river, there was no sign that Tom Sawyer Island had ever existed. By the time anyone had walked up to where the raft ride's entrance had been, it should have been abundantly obvious to them that the attraction was not available.

And yet, we kept a greeter here to reaffirm the obvious. Unfortunately, the old Tom Sawyer Island entrance, where were supposed to stand, was at the narrowest pinch point along that now-walled path. Not a great place to stop people and engage in friendly conversation about the park.

So we drifted down the path a bit, toward Frontierland. Unfortunately, that moved us closer to Pecos Bill's restaurants and the Turkey Leg wagon. We quickly discovered, after draining the river, that hundreds of Disney World guests had not chucked the turkey leg bones they'd been gnawing into one of the many trash cans provided, but into the river itself.

With the water drained, that exposed enough turkey bones to make the river bed look like a Jurassic fossil dig. The gamey muck also attracted every seagull between Jacksonville and Miami.

Can you see where this is going?

Unfortunately, the day it happened to me, I couldn't. I was standing at the corner of the river, trying to keep traffic moving to and from Thunder, when I felt someone nail me hard in the shoulder with a rock.

I wasn't standing underneath anything, so I knew that nothing could have fallen on me. Maybe some over-eager worker mucking out the river had hurled something over the wall? All I knew is that my shoulder hurt like heck. And... was I bleeding? It felt like something was seeping around where I'd been hit.

I jerked my head to the left to look at my shoulder... and found a dime-sized glop of bird poop.

How could something that small hurt so much? Slowly, as the stink filled my nose, I remembered Physics 101: even a small mass could pack a lot of force if it were moving fast enough. Stinky the Seagull must have relieved himself pretty far above me.

But what to do now? Fortunately, Disney's costume department stood ready to provide me a new shirt immediately and to wash the gunk off the old one. All it took was a quick trip into the Magic Kingdom tunnels and over to the wardrobe department for a fresh shirt. I guess I was lucky that the only time I've ever been nailed by a bird, I was working at Walt Disney World. (Though I was told afterward by a park old-timer that it wasn't unheard of for the wardrobe department to clean a guest's shirt in the same situation, if a supervisor took pity. Of course, most folks in that situation just bought a new T-shirt and dumped the fouled one.)

A *reader responds:*

I worked at SeaWorld. Closing the park provided an interesting job hazard. At dusk, all of the park's large birds would fly up into the trees for the night. Moving from place to place through the park was dangerous. There was no pathway at that time that WASN'T under a tree, now loaded with 20 or 30 very large birds - birds that had been eating popcorn and pretzels and other junk food all day rather than their normal, carefully regulated diets. We literally ran from one place to another, dodging the areas that had the heaviest bird populations that night. I never got completely nailed, but there were many close calls and more than enough "splash back" from the large birds!

When the construction of SeaWorld's new entryway began, we added a new level of danger. The construction wall effectively halved what was then the entrance. The pathway was at its narrowest right across from what was then the ice cream shop. Guests would come out of the shop with large waffle cones of ice cream, only to be greeted by 10 or 20 seagulls lined up on the fence. It was as if the gulls were planning their attacks : "You get this one Bernie, and the next one is mine!" Guests would be dive-bombed, usually resulting in the dropping of the precious treat on the pavement for the birds to attack. The ice cream shop gave away as many cones as they sold that summer!

How to have a horrible theme park vacation

Plenty of blog posts on the Internet will tell you how to get the most from your theme park vacation and enjoy your day. But who needs that? Not you, Mr. or Ms. Steel-Eyed-Realist. You want the *real* scoop on how to attack your vacation like a pit bull on a pile of raw steak. So I'm sending away the silly optimists now and letting you in on the secret. These tips are just for you:

Show up late in the morning

You're on vacation - of course you're going to sleep in! There's no need to get up early to visit a theme park. When the park opens, there are no lines, so how can you tell which rides are worth doing?

Wait to buy your tickets at the gate

Doing advance research online is confusing. It's for insecure people who don't make their best decisions under cold, hard pressure. That's not you. You live for the brash, last-minute decision. So queue up, ignore the signs and wait until you get to the window to decide which tickets to buy.

Eat lunch at noon

Sure, you've only been in the park for maybe an hour at this point, but who's going to tell you to deviate from your schedule? No one! It's noon, which is lunch time, so you're going to eat. No matter how long it takes.

Go on the rides with the longest lines, since they must be the best

Watch the crowd. See where they go, and follow them. That's how you'll find the best rides in the park.

Try to sneak your kids onto attractions they're too short to ride

You paid good money for those discounted kids' admission to the park, so they're entitled to go on every last ride in the place. Rules are for other people. Tell you kids to stand on their tippie-toes when the park employee measures them. That always works. And if it doesn't...

Complain, early and often

Every smart consumer knows that complaining, as loudly and with as much anger as possible, is how you get the best service. Demand to see a manager. Threaten to have everyone fired. Even better, threaten to write a negative review online. Now that's something that really motivates service workers to shape up and start doing their best!

Take extra time to take pictures of your whole family when you're getting on a ride

This is a special day, and you'll want to remember it forever. So be sure to take the time you need to get that special picture of everyone cramming onto every single ride vehicle all day long. It's the park's job to make sure you're having a good time, so they'll be happy to stop the ride for you, holding the line and keeping other riders from exiting while you compose that perfect shot.

Remember that if you're not waiting in line or riding, you're wasting your money

Rides are the only reason to visit a theme park, so if you're not on a ride or waiting for one, you're wasting your time and money. Taking a break in lush garden, dining in a charming, themed restaurant or resting on a park bench near the lake are time-wasters for suckers.

Yell at your kids

They're too young to know what's good for 'em, so if they start slacking, moaning or, heaven forbid, crying, let loose with your best drill sergeant impression and scream at them until they fall in line and obey you.

Buy lots of souvenirs and carry them around with you all day

You want people to know that you've got the money to afford this vacation. (Or, at least, that you did at the beginning of the day.) So carry around your bags and bags of souvenirs like the badges of honor that they are. Who cares how much it slows you down or tires the kids? Think of this as weight training! It's like gym class. Again, free package storage or delivery services are for wimps. Not smart folks like you.

So there you go, 10 tips designed to ensure that you get the theme park vacation you *truly* deserve.

Readers add:

Bring your two-week-old. The baby will love it and remember it for a lifetime. Especially in the summer.

Ignore advice about sunscreen. In fact, try to expose as much skin as possible. Especially if you are fat, fair-skinned and have lots of tattoos to show off.

Give cuts in line to your friends, and have them return the favor. After all, going for food, bathroom and drinks should give you an automatic exemption from waiting at the end of the line.

Talk on your cell phone the entire time you are in line. When you have nobody to call, check your Facebook and email every two minutes.

Get a stroller (even if you don't have kids). Use it as a battering ram to get you through crowds and to haul all the junk you were convinced you needed to bring into the park.

Smoke. Everyone loves getting second-hand-smoke-stink on their clothes and in their lungs. When anyone complains, get angry and complain about how your rights have been violated.

Get the biggest hat available in the park and wear it on every attraction, and especially to all the shows. Be sure to sit near the front when you do.

Always remember that you deserve the best seat in every theater. Don't worry about the cast member telling you to move all the way down the row, filling every available seat. That's for losers who don't know that you can only really enjoy the show from the seats in the exact center of the theater. People will not mind squeezing by you as the cast member keeps repeating the seating announcement over and over again. In fact, they will probably admire you for your tenacity.

Never, ever make reservations at park restaurants, especially on peak attendance days. You should be able to eat where you want, when you want. Yes, the lines may be long, but if you glare at the staff long enough and ask "How much longer will I have to wait?" every two minutes, they will almost certainly realize how important you are and seat you right away.

Don't forget to take as many flash photos as you want, especially on dark rides; people won't mind that it ruins the setting. Oh, and stop in the middle of pathways suddenly to read your map. Others will just walk around you.

Come unequipped: Don't bring a backpack or equivalent. They're heavy and unfashionable. Buy your water, lunch, dinner, snacks, sunscreen, pictures, hats, raincoats, and other necessities/amenities at the park. The price is right, plus the foodstuffs pack all the nutritional value you need to tackle a 14-hour aerobic exercise. If it rains, you'll have an excuse to buy one of those cool ponchos the parks sell. Then you can take your newest purchase on the water rides to avoid getting wet. It just makes sense.

Wait until you're at the front of a 20-minute line to decide what to buy. Sure, they only sell two entrées - a burger with or without cheese - but you need a second opinion! Your family members have always asked for cheese on their burgers for the past 15 years, but maybe they've incurred lactose-intolerance in the last few minutes. Don't bother getting out your wallet beforehand. You work better under pressure. Oops! You don't have cash. They probably take Amex. Nope? Well, surely they take traveller's checks. Nope? That's okay - your wife will be back from the washroom any minute now with cash. Lightheartedly apologize to the people behind you. "These idiots don't take Amex or traveler's checks!"

Make sure you and all your family members walk arm-in-arm regardless of the width of the walkway or amount of people, especially around parade routes.

Feel free to shove your kids to the curb two minutes before parades and then play the "I am just trying to get to my kids" routine. Much like not having reservations at restaurants, getting to the parade route early is overrated. As an alternative, if you are 6'4", having kids on your shoulders in the front row will encourages many around you to communicate with you.

Enter through the clearly marked exit, never mind those folks coming through the gate towards you. Surely these things will go both ways.

Similar to the food decisions mentioned earlier, get in line to purchase tickets. Then, when arriving at the teller, have a loud conversation – if possible, involving cell phones – about which ticket plan/combo to get.

Here are some fun games to play with your family while you wait in line to enter the park. When you get to the ticket entrance scanner:

- Make sure your kids pick any finger they want to scan the first time the tickets are used and do not watch. Why ruin the surprise? Imagine all the attention your kids will get, hopping from park to park as the attendants all but fingerprint their entire hand on the scanner.

- Thereafter hand out the thumb scanned-tickets to different family members. Have a camera ready to capture the magic.

Doing the right thing, when others do the wrong thing

Typically, I liked to make eye contact with the people standing at the front of my raft as I pushed it off from the Frontierland dock for our trip over to Tom Sawyer Island - the better for cracking a joke or answering a quick question. But in the case of one particular family, no one would look me in the eye. Instead, they just looked past me, back toward Frontierland.

Weird, I thought.

Perhaps it was some cultural thing. These Walt Disney World visitors looked Indian, and I wasn't then as used to dealing with people from elsewhere around the world as I am now. Wanting to keep the raft moving, I didn't linger, but walked to the back of the raft to put it into gear.

Then I heard the yell.

The formerly silent family came alive, waving their arms and calling. I looked over toward the street and saw an elderly woman, wearing a sari, return their wave and hurry down toward the dock.

Well, I thought, that explains why they were looking that way. They were missing a family member. But now they've gotten her attention, and she knows to catch the next raft over to the island.

All's well now, right?

Except that she kept running toward the dock.

No, she couldn't...

One of her family, on the front of the raft, unhooked the rope that blocked the entrance to the raft during its trip. The woman lowered her head and sped up.

This is not happening, I thought.

She couldn't be crazy enough to jump. The raft was a good six feet from the dock now, and moving away from it. An older woman in a sari wasn't exactly the sort of person one would expect to clear that distance.

Nor would her family be crazy enough to urge her on. Didn't anyone in the family have enough respect for Grandma to want to keep her from any chance of ending up in the river, while a engine prop whirred a few feet from her head?

Welcome to another of life's gut-check moments. Procedurally, I was doing everything right: I'd delivered my safety spiel, followed the correct cast-off procedure and even now offered a friendly holler at the woman to wait for the next raft.

But what good does following the rules do if it leaves you with Grandma in the drink?

Sure, if I kept going and the woman missed the jump, she'd be at fault for ignoring my warning as well as basic, common sense. But Disney's first rule (and the first rule at any other major park I know) is to keep the guests safe.

So I swung the raft's bow back toward the mainland, bringing it within a few inches of the dock as the woman hopped aboard the raft.

Her family cheered, then turned to wave at me. A few hollered a thank you.

I clenched my teeth and squeezed out a smile in return. I wanted to yell at the family for putting a loved one at risk, but that wasn't my job. My job was to keep that family - and everyone else visiting my attraction that day - safe and happy.

But when we made it to the other side, I couldn't help but say something.

"You know, we could have gotten you on the next raft," I said with a smile to Grandma.

Her family exploded in laughter.

"She never waits for anyone," one of them leaned over to tell me, with a shrug, as he walked off the raft.

Laughing together, they walked up the path into the island. Safe, and happy.

I'd done my job - I guess.

When VIPs go MIA

If you spend enough time at a major theme park like those at the Walt Disney World Resort, you're going to meet some celebrities. I once watched the Country Bear Jamboree next to George Lucas at the Magic Kingdom. I made change for Dustin Hoffman at the Shootin' Arcade, loaded Michael Jackson and his entourage onto a boat at Pirates of the Caribbean, and watched a young Alexa Ray Joel play with a couple of cast members while her dad, Billy, and his band rode Big Thunder Mountain Railroad.

But my favorite celebrity story appeals to the political science major in me. One late night at Pirates, about an hour before close, I was working as the lead, hanging out in the control tower talking about who knows what.

The cast member working load called me on the intercom: "Um, there's a VIP hostess here who's looking for the VIP corridor."

At Pirates, like at many other attractions, we had a VIP, or "back door," entrance through which tour guides could bring celebrities and other individuals whom Disney management allowed to bypass the regular queue. But rarely did VIP tours come through after 10pm. And when they did, the tour host usually knew better than to bother with the VIP entrance. If there's no one in the regular queue, what's the point of skipping it?

I suspected that the VIP hostess had been told to take her charges through the VIP entrance, so, dadgum it, that's what she was going to do.

If only she had known where it was.

So I walked down the steps to the queue and met the hostess, figuring that I'd just direct them to one of the empty boats we were cycling through the ride. But as soon as I found her, I realized that wasn't going to work.

"Hi, I'm Robert," I said to her, noticing that something important was missing from the scene. "Uh... so where's your VIP?"

"Oh, he got tired of walking. So he's sitting on a bench back in the queue."

Now, I never trained as a VIP host, but I'm pretty sure that the one thing you weren't supposed to do was leave your VIP in a public area while you wandered off. So I started, briskly, walking up the queue.

"Perhaps we should find him then," I said to her, doing my Disney best to avoid adding, "you idiot."

We turned three corners, and there, sitting with his wife in the middle of an empty Pirates of the Caribbean queue was Jacques Chirac, the then-mayor of Paris and former prime minister of France, whom I knew from my political science classes at Northwestern was tipped by many to be the next President of France (which he did become in 1995).

"Bonjour, Monsieur Chirac," I said to him, having no idea if this was appropriate - either diplomatically or grammatically. But, hey, the guy ran a NATO country and was sitting in my queue. I figured it rude not to suck up and say hi.

He stood up to shake my hand, responding in French, so I had to 'fess up.

"Uh, that's all the French I know. Sorry. Would you like to follow me onto the ride?"

Ignoring the VIP hostess, I swept my arm toward the passageway, in the direction of the loading platform, and started walking. The Chiracs followed, with the hostess trailing. The Chiracs chatted between themselves, in French, a conversation that I imagined went something like:

"Ah, I am so impressed by this intelligent young man! What an excellent leader he will be someday!"

But, probably, went something more like:

"Who the hell are Mickey and Minnie McClueless here, and why does it take both of them to get us on a friggin' empty amusement park ride? EuroDisney is so going to blow, by the way."

A reader responds:

A friend has worked in characters for years. She has played a variety of different characters including Mickey Mouse. Over the years she has made appearances with a bunch of celebrities who have visited the parks. On one occasion, the performer she appeared with was Dolly Parton.

Now everyone who has seen the character costumes understands that the size of the heads requires the performer inside to be aware of the proximity of the objects and people around them. When a character is posing for photos with children they are constantly working to be aware of what is around them -- so they don't turn too quickly and bump into someone or something ...

... Or in this case, some things.

At the appearance, Ms. Parton was to walk to the center of the stage alone. Then Minnie was to skip over to Dolly from stage left, and Mickey was to skip over from stage right. Dolly was to turn to Minnie and very slightly bow to Minnie, who would curtsy. Dolly would then turn to Mickey, again bow slightly and Mickey would bow in return.

Now to add a little more "magic" to the story: The whole production was for a press event -- meaning the front row was wall-to-wall photographers.

Out came Dolly. Out skipped Minnie. Out skipped Mickey. Ms. Parton turned to Minnie and bowed to her curtsy. She turned to Mickey (my friend) who had lost a bit of her awareness about where the head was.

Dolly bowed and Mickey bowed -- placing his nose squarely into Ms. Parton's cleavage.

My friend realized she had bumped into something (again "things"). But when she pulled back what she remembered was about a million camera flashes blowin' up from the press.

Her Minnie (who later backstage laughed uncontrollably) played it off, crossing her arms and stomping her yellow pumps.

You never know whom you'll meet on a parade route

My younger sister was the first in our family to work at the Walt Disney World Resort, taking a job at the old Troubador Tavern drink station in the Magic Kingdom shortly after my family moved from Indianapolis to Orlando. But as soon as she turned 18, she quickly transferred out of foods and into attractions, starting as a hostess in the Enchanted Tiki Room in the Magic Kingdom's Adventureland.

As most attractions cast members do from time to time, she was sent over to work crowd (excuse me, "guest") control on the parade route on some afternoons. Here's her favorite parade route story.

The parade route crosses through Liberty Square and Frontierland on the park's west side. Those two areas don't have quite enough cast members to handle the parade crowd, so Adventureland cast members such as my sister were called in. Her job that day was to keep traffic flowing around the crosswalks in Frontierland.

Most of the time, this just meant hanging out and answering guest questions. But at 15 minutes until parade time, she was supposed to start clearing the parade route. That meant standing at a crosswalk, facing the direction that the parade would be moving, and telling people to please move behind the ropes and off the parade route.

For the first 10 minutes or so, she was pretty mellow about the request. If people kept walking on the route there was plenty of time for cast members at crosswalks farther up the route to catch them. No need to provoke an unpleasant confrontation at the "happiest place on Earth," after all. It was only in the last five minutes or so before the appearance of the first parade unit that she got serious about keeping everyone off the parade route.

And I do mean *everyone*.

So when my sister saw an elderly man walking toward her along the route, she sprang into action. She'd noticed many people in the crowd staring at the man walking the wrong way up the parade route, so she wondered why it hadn't occurred to him yet that he might be doing something wrong, with so many people watching him and pointing his way.

"Excuse me, sir," she said in her best Disney voice, with her wide, friendly smile. "Could you please move behind the ropes?"

Immediately, two men in dark suits and sunglasses appeared at her sides.

"He can keep moving," one hissed quietly in her ear. The elderly man walked past my sister, returning a smile that was even wider and friendlier than my sister's.

The two men in suits were gone. My sister turned to her partner at the crosswalk, who stared at her in horror.

"Don't you know who that was?" she asked.

"No," my sister replied, wondering what the fuss was over this one elderly man, among hundreds of others, in the Magic Kingdom.

"That was Jimmy Carter," the other cast member said.

And for all the years since, I've teased my sister that I could recognize the mayor of Paris, but she spaced her encounter with a former President of the United States.

What time is the three o'clock parade?

It's become a long-running joke among Disney cast members - the question that, inevitably, you hear any time you work a location on or near the Magic Kingdom parade route: "What time is the three o'clock parade?"

For many, the question illustrates what they consider to be the vacation-induced stupidity of theme park guests. I mean, c'mon, they just answered their question in the question. The parade's at three o'clock. Duh.

But as satisfying as it might seem to think yourself smarter than all those tourists out there, as a cast member, it's not your job to put people down. Quite the opposite, in fact. It's your job to do whatever you can to help them feel like they're having the best day of their lives.

So... no mocking the guests for asking the time of the three o'clock parade. Just fire up that Disney smile and give 'em the answer.

"3:15," I replied, when asked one day early in my Walt Disney World career.

I hadn't mean to say anything other than "3:00," but for some reason, I felt like I should respond with the time that the parade would pass the point where we were standing in Frontierland, instead of the time when the parade first stepped off on Main Street. (The afternoon parades back then stared on Main Street and proceeded around the hub and into Liberty Square before ending in Frontierland.)

The guest smiled and turned back toward his family, happy with my answer.

He'd known that the three o'clock parade started on Main Street at three o'clock. He wasn't the idiot that some short-sighted cast members made folks like him out to be. What that guest really wanted to know, and inelegantly asked, was "at what time does the three o'clock parade get here?"

Reflexively, I'd given him the correct answer.

Lesson learned. The answer you should give as a cast member isn't always to the question the guest asks. The answer you should give is to the question that the guest meant to ask.

From then on, I treated guest questions like I was Encyclopedia Brown on a case: Each one was a potential mystery to be unraveled, then solved.

Turns out that a woman entering Pirates of the Caribbean who asked "Is this ride okay for kids?" really wanted to know if there were any snakes on the ride, because she had a phobia.

A couple who asked "How long does this ride take?" when boarding my Tom Sawyer Island raft didn't care how long it'd take me to drive the thing across the river. They wanted to know when they'd have to be back to the island-side dock so that they would make their 1:30 Diamond Horseshoe reservations.

Deciphering a guest question properly can save more than a restaurant reservation. A man outside Country Bear Jamboree who asked me, "Where can I rent a wheelchair?" really meant "My grandmother's passed out from the heat and could you call us a nurse, please?" (Fortunately, I figured that one out almost immediately, and had a medical unit on the way within seconds.)

What time is the three o'clock parade? Maybe it's at 3:15, or 3:25, depending where you're standing when asked. Or maybe the correct answer is "I'm sorry, sir, but the parade doesn't come here into Tomorrowland." Or even, "You'll hear an announcement if the parade is delayed or cancelled due to the weather."

There are no stupid questions, not when you take the time to discover what the guest really wants to know.

To all my Brazilian girlfriends

She was part of a Brazilian tour group - you could tell from the gold and green T-shirt that she wore, the same worn by hundreds of other teens in the Magic Kingdom that day. She walked up to me slowly, almost stumbling, glancing nervously back over her shoulder toward her friend with each step. They giggled.

"Picture?" she asked me, holding a camera in her hand.

Having done this, oh, about ten thousand times before, I immediately answered "yes" and reached for the camera, figuring I'd be taking a picture of the two teen girls.

Not so fast. The second girl sprang forward to snatch the camera, as the first girl turned and pasted herself to my side. Smile, flash, and they were gone. Giggling.

The other cast member working with me chuckled.

"So, what's your girlfriend's name?"

"Huh?"

"Your new Brazilian girlfriend."

"I've never seen her before in my life. I have no idea even what her name is," I replied.

The other cast member threw back her head and laughed so loudly that some of the people waiting for that night's Electrical Parade turned to look.

"That's not what she's going to tell her friends back home!"

Walking the theme park power walk

You think it's frustrating walking through a crowded theme park on a busy summer day?

Try walking through those crowds while the 15 minutes of your precious sit-down, air-conditioned break are ticking away.

Every new theme park employee faces this problem. You go on break for the first time, then waste 10 minutes of your break wading through the crowd to get to, and then back from, the break room. (Or the cafeteria.) That's why theme park employees develop what I call the "theme park power walk."

It's the ability to walk through a theme park crowd like a kayaker steers through Class IV rapids. You watch the crowd to see how fast it's flowing, go with the swiftest stream, then keep your eyes open for obstacles downstream that you'll need to steer around.

The biggest mistake people make when trying to navigate a theme park crowd is looking at the bodies in front of them. Look at their heads, instead. Stay with those looking straight ahead, and prepare to swing around those who move their gaze to either side. They'll soon stop or slow down, throwing the current around them into turmoil.

Strollers are the jagged boulders of the theme park rapids. Swing well away from them.

Big groups are trouble, too. If one person in the group gets distracted, all will slow or stop. Find the people walking alone, eager to get to their destination, and slice through the crowd with them.

I laugh when people try to run in theme parks. Forget the rules prohibiting it. Runners are like those sports cars on the highway that rush up to pass the next car, never noticing the slower traffic ahead that's going to force them to eat their brakes. A good power walker, keeping his or her eyes on the current flowing ahead, will beat a runner through the crowd almost every time.

Of course, my power walk drives my family nuts when I bring them to a park. My wife worked one summer at Epcot, but she was "talent" (in the Disney All-American College Orchestra) and rarely had to get through the park alone, so she never developed "the walk." My wife and kids hang back like "civilians," wondering why I'm plowing through the crowd when I'm supposed to be on vacation and relaxed.

Hey, old habits die hard. Plus, I've got a ride to get to!

A *reader replies:*

People should learn to walk like they drive their car. Correction: people should walk like they *should* drive their car:

Always have consideration for people trying to overtake you. Check over your shoulder before you make a wild turn. Slowing down, check back to make sure no ones going to rear end you.

I learned the power walk many years ago when I worked sideshows at the Palace Pier in Brighton, United Kingdom. I had a 15-minute break to walk half a mile from the attractions to the end of the pier, via a food vendor, begging people to hurry up and make their selection, then eat and walk back again.

My trick is not to watch the people in front of me, but the people in front of them. Plan ahead and make decisions early. Walking against the flow of traffic sometimes works better because they see you coming and move when they see the angst in your face to get through.

A white-knuckle ride on 'Body Wars'

One of the great perks of working in a theme park is the opportunity to be among the first to ride its new attractions. I took advantage of that opportunity – the few times I had it – starting with the opening of Body Wars in the old Wonders of Life pavilion at Epcot in 1989.

With so many simulator rides now in theme parks, museums and even shopping malls, it might be hard for some to remember what a big deal they were back in the 1980s. Star Tours debuted at Disneyland in 1987, and it was such an immediate hit that the park stayed open for 60 hours straight to accommodate the crowds.

The simulator was the most revolutionary new ride experience for theme parks since the introduction of roller coaster inversions in the 1970s. Body Wars was to be the Orlando area's first simulator ride. (The east-coast version of Star Tours would not open at the then-Disney-MGM Studios for another few months.) So of course I switched a shift in order to be at Epcot the first afternoon the ride was open to cast member previews.

To my delight, I found that Body Wars was, thematically, a souped-up version of my beloved "Adventure Through Inner Space," the long-closed attraction that was my one "must ride" whenever I visited

Disneyland as a child. Like on that ride, we'd be shrunk down to the size of a blood cell, zipping through the circulation system – this time to save a wounded patient.

Cool.

So I walked into the simulator, took the seat in the far back corner, and buckled in.

Way cool.

The cabin lights dimmed, and the theater itself began to buck forward.

Inexplicably way cool.

And, then, as the theater whipped to the side and we began our chase, my seatbelt unfastened.

Not cool.

At that moment, I first understood the origin of the phrase "white knuckle ride." The blood drained from my fingers as I pressed my hands into the armrests, trying to get enough leverage to push my back into the seat as the Body Wars theater treated me like a wet pair of jeans in a dryer spin cycle.

I tried to refasten the belt, but thought better of it when the ride whipped to the side as I began take my hand off the armrest. Nope, I'd have to hold on for this flight.

And, remember, I'd never been on a simulator ride before. Today, if the same thing were to happen, I'd know how the ride would behave and better be able to react. But then, I had no clue.

Pitch. Yaw. Roll.

Clutch. Press. Pray.

Later, once I was safely off the ride and the nausea finally had gone away, I learned that the back corner seats typically get the widest range of motion on simulator rides. (If you're a newbie and want to take it easy, try to get a seat in the middle of the theater. And, oh yeah, they fixed the thing with the seat belts.) A maintenance tech also later told me that Body Wars ran on its highest motion levels those first couple days of cast member testing, and that Disney dialed down the range of motion substantially before the ride opened to the public.

I don't know if he was feeding me a line. But I do know that I've never had as much of a thrill on a simulator attraction as I did on that very first ride, on Body Wars.

A reader replies:

These days the seat belt sensors would definitely be tied into the control system, but in those days it was a manual system, checked before departure, and the belt sensor was able to make contact a tiny bit before actually latching.

You're correct, the motion was dialed back after a short period because it was making nearly everyone sick. Unlike Star Tours, there weren't a lot of good visual references, and the motion was quite rhythmic. The result was almost guaranteed to create nausea.

The one with the security camera

In answer to a couple of popular questions about working at the Walt Disney World Resort:

"Are there really security cameras everywhere at Walt Disney World?"

Well, I wouldn't say that they are everywhere, but Disney uses security cameras in many of its attractions.

"Have you ever seen, well, you know...?"

Yes.

"But I didn't say what I meant."

Doesn't matter. Whatever you meant, we've seen it happening on a security camera at Disney World.

Here's the warning: Bail out of this story now if you're easily offended.

Still here? Oh-kay. Let's proceed.

It was parade time in the afternoon, during one of the slower months of the year in the Magic Kingdom. I was sitting in the control tower at Pirates of the Caribbean and our line had evaporated, as almost everyone in this side of the park had made their way over to Frontierland for the parade. The only people still in our queue was a young couple, a man and a woman in their late teens or early 20s. They got into a boat, alone. Nothing but empty boats around them.

I knew that they were aware of this, too, because both of them were looking around at the empty boats as they drifted away from the loading platform.

"Why is she looking around so much?" another Pirate cast member asked as he walked through the tower control room.

I arched an eyebrow and smirked.

"Oh," he replied, as two other cast members overheard us, then walked in from the adjacent break room.

All eyes turned to the bank of video monitors in front of us. Sure enough, as the boat approached the flume drop in Hurricane Cove, where the camera looked at the passing boats from behind, we saw not two bodies in the boat, but one.

"Where'd she go?" the first cast member asked, innocently. The rest of us arched eyebrows this time, in response. One cast member rushed back into the break room and picked up the phone.

"Hey, yeah, this is Mark at Pirates. We've got a hot one in the monitors here...."

I'm not proud of what I did next. Rather than leave the couple to, uh, enjoy their ride, I decided to interrupt the fun for a moment. With my left hand, I flipped a switch on the console, activating the boat stop at the top of the drop. That triggers a pair of metal plates to swing into the ride flume at that point, catching the front wheels underneath the boat, stopping it from going over the drop.

With a bump, the boat stopped, suddenly. The young lady's head popped up, now visible in the screen.

"Oooo," a couple of the male cast members exhaled, wincing, thinking about where she was at the moment of impact. Like I said, I'm not proud.

"Oh, there she is," replied the cast member who'd asked, turning as red as our pirate vests.

I released the boat stop, sending the couple plunging into the abyss.

There are no security cameras in the battle scene, so we couldn't see what the couple was, uh, up to, for the next couple of minutes. But just before they re-emerged in the chase scene's camera, the door to the control tower burst open.

In rushed two supervisors and what seemed like an entire crew of Jungle Cruise skippers. All gathered around the monitors. No one said a word.

No one needed to. We all knew why they were here.

We watched empty boat after empty boat enter the chase scene. And then, our friends returned. From the angle of the camera in the chase scene, we got a full frontal view of the action in our grainy black-and-white monitor.

Silence, all around. Then, from the back of the now-crowded small control room, a giggle.

Then another.

Then, laughter erupted all around. Several of the Pirate cast members rushed out of the room, down the staircase toward the unload platform. A couple of the Jungle skippers stepped to follow, before a supervisor grabbed one by the collar. Oh yeah, Jungle skippers aren't supposed to be seen by the public inside Pirates of the Caribbean.

The couple was out of camera view in the burning city, but within a minute they would arrive at the unload station. In the camera monitor, I saw the cast members who'd run out of the control room gather around the podium in the unload station. Back in the tower, the cast member standing next to me pulled the microphone toward him.

"You're not," I said to him.

"Of course I am," he replied, with a wide grin, as he pushed the button to activate the unload station speaker.

The couple arrived, sitting quietly and composed in their boat, as if nothing unusual had happened. But as they stepped up to leave, my colleague on the mic spoke.

"For your safety, this has been a camera-monitored attraction."

The young lady put her hands over her face and ran from the unload platform. Her boyfriend? He looked at the welcoming committee... and smiled as he strutted out of the room. The cast members applauded.

The supervisors shooed the Jungle cast members back to their attraction and I looked up at the clock. My shift ended five minutes ago. With the post-parade rush of guests now flooding into Adventureland, I walked out quickly, to avoid getting caught in the crowd.

About 10 minutes later, I'd changed into my regular clothes and was waiting for the parking lot shuttle bus outside the tunnel entrance behind It's a Small World. Several cast members whom I knew worked on the east-side, at Space Mountain and the Speedway, were talking excitedly as we boarded the bus. I overheard them.

"Did you hear what happened at Pirates today?"

Grad Night Police of the Caribbean

Crouched behind a fake rock, I watched the boats pass, one by one. My eyes had adjusted to the lack of light. The flashlight in my hand? I carried it not to help me see, but so that I could be seen.

When the time came.

I smelled the boat before I saw it. As the crew of teenagers rounded corner of Hurricane Cove, I waited for, then saw, the glowing tip of the joint. Row four.

Flashlight on. Panic.

As my flashlight illuminated the boat of Grad Night partiers, it also shone directly into the security camera mounted on the wall directly behind them. The cast member in tower would see the light, and deploy the boat stop that would trap the passengers in front of me.

The boat hit the stop, and the passengers lurched forward. The kid dropped his joint. His girlfriend shrieked, then slapped him across the shoulder. I doubt he felt it, or even heard her. His eyes opened, wide, toward me.

His friend, sitting on his other side, craned his neck forward a touch. He squinted at me. Maybe he was trying to lighten the moment with a joke.

"Dude," (I swear he actually said "Dude"), "that pirate looks so real."

Or maybe he was just stoned.

Many veteran Walt Disney World cast members avoid working Grad Nights. They don't like the late-night hours, or the hassle of enforcing order among tens of thousands of only-theoretically supervised teenagers.

Me? Not yet a year out of college, I couldn't wait for the opportunity to scare the living excrement out of some high school kids.

On Grad Nights, we stationed extra cast members to work "audience control" along parade routes and in attraction queues. We also stationed cast members inside some of the longer, slower rides, including Pirates of the Caribbean. We'd learned from experience that many kids thought they weren't being watched while on the ride, so they saw these rides as their best chance to get away with smoking/drinking/uh, whatever.

So we waited for them. Flashlights in hand. Ready to use the most awesome weapon imaginable to destroy a teenager:

Embarrassment.

"Hand it over."

The girlfriend yanked on Smokey McPuff's arm, glaring at him, which also served to turn her face away from me. Smokey pulled a small plastic sandwich bag from his pocket. Two kids from the front row handed up a flask. I hadn't even seen them. Bonus. I dragged my flashlight across each row, to see what else I could find.

No one would make eye contact with me. Except for Smokey and his buddy, who still seemed to be trying to figure out if I was real.

Not wanting to hold up the ride too long, I waved my flashlight forward, signaling tower to release the stop and drop the boat down the waterfall.

The nearly empty sandwich bag and half-empty flask would end up with Magic Kingdom security, which over the course of the evening would collect enough contraband to fill the limo of a rock star on his way to check into "Celebrity Rehab."

The rest of the night, I tried to fight the boredom as boat after boat after boat of normal, perfectly well-behaved kids floated past. After a while, what I was doing reminded me of fishing. Hour after hour, you sit there, staring at the water. You learn every detail of the place. You notice every ripple in the water, every reed on the bank.

Every last blasted verse of "Yo Ho, A Pirate's Life for Me."

But every once in a long while, the line snaps... and you catch something.

Going overboard at Pirates of the Caribbean

Hourly capacity is the Holy Grail of the theme park business. The more people you can put through an attraction in one hour, the shorter its line will be. The more people a park's attraction can put through, the more rides you can go on in one day. So, high hourly capacity = happy customers.

It shouldn't surprise you then to learn that Disney runs some of the highest capacity rides in the business. When I worked at the Magic Kingdom, the highest capacity ride on our side of the park was Pirates of Caribbean. We could put more than 2,000 people per hour through Pirates, without breaking much of a sweat.

But one summer, our hourly numbers were lagging. Counts dipped below 2,000, to 1,800 - then 1,600 - per hour, and our mid-day wait time was creeping over one hour.

In those days, Pirates loaded boats in two side-by-side channels, which merged as the boats made a right turn into the upper grotto. Slow boats would linger there, allowing the boat from the other channel to catch up and pinch it at the merge point, stopping both boats and forcing attraction operators to come down and pull the two boats apart. That delay slowed the flow of boats (and guests) into the ride, crippling the hourly count.

So what was management's solution?

To put the most experienced operators at the load and tower positions at peak periods, to better time the dispatch of boats? No.

To increase the volume of the ride pumps at the merge point, to blast more water and make the boats flow faster? Nope.

Management's solution was... to put a cast member in the water at the merge point, to push the boats faster through the ride.

Only male cast members were allowed into the water, as our Pirates costumes included shoes. (Ladies who worked Pirates wore their own black character shoes, and Disney didn't want to have to pay for employees' shoes that were ruined by getting wet.) We wore chest-high rubber waders that someone borrowed from maintenance, and would give each boat a shove as it drifted by.

To get into the water, we'd have to stop the line at load, get into an empty boat and ride to the merge point. There, we'd hop over the side and into the water, while the person we were relieving would climb back in, for the ride back around to unload. You had to be very careful to go over the side of the boat, and not the front or the back. That way, you'd stay outside the ride flume, because if you got into the water inside the ride flume, well... as they say, dead men tell no tales.

Now, one could question the wisdom of taking a boat out of commission every half hour to do the switch, when we were trying to increase the number of guests in the ride. But, hey, given the number of work safety rules this little scheme was violating, it should have been clear that wisdom wasn't exactly in play here. (Pirates of the Caribbean's Standard Operating Procedure was explicit that all water pumps had to be turned off before any cast member could enter the water. Oh, well.)

Did it work? Supervisors eagerly checked our numbers throughout the day. And the hourly counts did tick up a bit, usually when less-experienced cast members went into the water, leaving the more experienced ones to work load and tower.

After a few weeks, though, word came down one morning - do not get into the water. The waders were removed from the Pirates office, and the leads told the operators not to bother asking if we were going to do that again. We all suspected that a manager "higher up the chain" got word of what was happening, freaked out, and ordered the pushing stopped. Immediately.

Later that week, a couple of us decided to address the hourly capacity problem our own way. A cast member named Ben and I "froze" ourselves at the two loading positions for two hours, telling everyone else to bump around us. A cast member named Mark did the same in tower. For those two hours, we worked as a slick machine, filling boats and dispatching them smoothly, with no merge point problems. The hourly counts? More than 2,800 guests per hour.

Today, Pirates at the Magic Kingdom loads in a single channel, eliminating the merge point issue. And I've heard that it often runs more than the 24 boats that we usually ran back in my day. But good, experienced cast members at the load position can still help boost the hourly count and draw down a line, at Pirates or any other attraction.

A *reader responds:*

It was one of the hottest summers on record at Universal Studios Hollywood, probably 1988 or 1989. Trams were backed up all over the backlot, so the tram loading area was really, really backed up. The actual wait in line, even after you brought your boarding pass, was at least two hours (these are the days before any "rides," kids... just the stunt shows and the tram tour).

One manager was convinced that all the situation needed was some entertainment, a costumed character to placate the near-rioting guests. He got on the radio and broadcast to everyone within earshot, "We've got a bad situation here. Send in the Wolfman."

To this day, many of my friends, ex-co-workers and I (and, from what I hear, even some folks who still work at the tour) use the term "send in the Wolfman" when things are at their most ridiculously dire.

Sometimes, Mother Nature runs the show

Starting from when you board the ferry at the Transportation and Ticket Center and sail across the Seven Seas Lagoon, all the way through your day in the Magic Kingdom, whether you take a boat around the Rivers of America or ascend Big Thunder, every body of water you see and every landscape you cross will be 100-percent, completely, totally man-made.

But from time to time, Mother Nature reminds cast members they cannot completely dismiss her will. The afternoon thunderstorms provide one example. We often found other examples, working the rafts at Tom Sawyer Island.

The island rarely failed to open at its designated time each morning when I worked there. The rafts typically opened an hour after the park, partly because it wasn't exactly the most popular attraction in the Magic Kingdom, but mostly because no work could be done on the island, to stock the restaurant or do any required maintenance work, until the sun came up. Unlike every other location in the park, the island had no artificial street light, which is why the island closes at dusk. With no artificial lights for the third shift, work had to wait until sun-up, so we waited until 10 am to open the island to guests.

The lead still showed up at 7:30, though, as he or she would be needed to ferry some of the maintenance and food workers across the river. Custodial had a Jon boat that they used to take trash off the island, but everyone else relied on the rafts. I arrived for my lead shift several minutes early one morning, carrying the box of doughnuts and the morning paper that I used as bait to ensure both that my morning crew would be on time, and that supervisors would drop in, when I could confront them with the list of show quality repairs that I wanted approved.

But as soon as I turned the corner onto the Tom Sawyer Island rafts' mainland dock, I immediately knew that this wouldn't be a normal morning on the island.

Not with a very large alligator - and her kids - sunning themselves on the dock.

I froze and hid the doughnuts behind my back (I have no idea whether gators like doughnuts, and had no inclination to find out). Slowly, I backed up. I walked the long way around the raft dock cabin, so I could get into the office within it from the queue's exit.

I called animal control.

"Um, we've got three alligators on the Tom Sawyer Island raft dock. Could you send someone down?"

"On the island or the mainland?"

"Mainland."

"Oooookay."

While I waited for animal control, I called the opening supervisor. No need for doughnuts today, I figured I'd soon have every suit in the Magic Kingdom on my dock, regardless.

Well, not actually on the dock, just near it – a respectable distance away. But they'd be looking at the dock.

Within five minutes, I was hosting a little morning get-together for two animal control guys, two attractions supervisors, the area manager, and a merchandise supervisor who walked over to see what the fuss was about.

One of the attractions supervisors turned to one of the animal control guys.

"So, how soon can you move those alligators so that we can open?"

The animal control guys exploded with laughter.

"Sorry, we don't move gators. They get to stay as loooong as they want."

The attractions supervisors looked a bit queasy.

"You want to know when you'll be open?" the other animal control guy asked, as he nodded toward the attractions supervisors. "Go on down and ask the gator!"

When the park opened that morning, Tom Sawyer Island became Disney's Gatorland, and the raft drivers became crowd control, managing the flow of guests who lined up along the riverside walkway to gawk at Mrs. Gator and her young-'uns. Around 10:15, the gators had had enough. They slipped into the water and swam away.

We waited another 20 minutes before we opened the ride. Just in case the gators decided to come back.

Because, you know, sometimes Mother Nature runs the show.

Drowning under short-term thinking

Standard operating procedure for the Tom Sawyer Island rafts dictated that the maximum number of people one should load on a raft is 55.

The most I ever packed onto a raft? Ninety.

Hey, why not pack on more? People have been waiting 10-15 minutes, or more, to get on a raft. As long as there's space, why not have a few more board?

Just ask people to push in tighter, to allow a few more people to get across on this raft. After all, the more people you get on a raft, the more people you can get out of the line, and the shorter everyone's wait will be, right?

Working in a theme park, one learns that what seems obvious in the short term may turn out to be a really bad decision on a grand scale. It seemed like a good idea to pack people into our rafts like a Kardashian in a cocktail dress. Sure, people might be uncomfortable for that minute or two crossing the river, but it keeps the line down, right?

Actually, it doesn't. What happens when you load almost twice as many people on a Tom Sawyer Island raft than it was designed to carry? Well, it sinks.

Not all the way (at least not while I was driving). But the raft does start to take on water, enough so that the people riding up front start climbing up the rails on the side of the raft to keep their feet from getting wet.

Heck, we even had a hand signal that cast members working the river attractions could use to tell a Tom Sawyer Island raft driver that his front end was taking on water. (Hold you hand over your head, palm down, and pass the hand back and forth over your head.) When you saw the signal, you were supposed to slow down. At full speed, the water coming over the front created additional downforce on the front of the raft, causing it to take on even more water. Slow down, and some of that water would slide over the sides; the raft could straighten out a bit, and you could crawl across the river with less water rushing onto the raft.

See the problem now? With more people on the raft, we had to drive across the river much more slowly than with a properly loaded raft.

Eventually, the light bulb turned on in my brain, and I decided to run an experiment. For one hour, we counted the people coming onto the rafts, and cut the load at 55 people. (This required stopping folks at around 45-50 and then asking for party counts, so that we didn't go over 55.) Then, we'd go back to the old way the next hour, then see how many people we put through each hour.

The results stunned me. Running the lighter loads, we put through almost 40 percent more people.

Not only could we cross the river more quickly because we were running lighter rafts and not having to slow down for water, we were spending far less time in dock, since we weren't spending time asking people to pack themselves in to get a full (over)load. It was just load and go. Even though we were carrying fewer people per raft, we were able to make so many more crossings that our overall numbers were way up.

And no one got his or her feet wet.

A few times during our experiment, the family with person number 56 would complain - pointing out a bit of extra space on the raft and asking, why they couldn't cram aboard, too? When we held to our new policy, responding with a smile and a "the next raft will be here in just a minute" while casting off, the numbers stayed up. But when we acquiesced, then the person behind that party wanted on, too, and soon we were back to overloaded rafts, extra minutes in dock... and slow crossings with wet feet. So we stuck with the "light load" policy.

That summer, the Magic Kingdom West supervisors were running a contest among the area's attractions - the one with the best performance in guest counts, guest compliments and "secret shopper" evaluations, would win. When we were overloading the rafts the old way, Tom Sawyer Island stood in last place among the attractions on our side of the park. After changing our load policy, we soon moved into first place, and we ultimately won the competition.

For what it's worth, that summer on Tom Sawyer Island taught me a lesson that changed the way I think about life in general: Look at the big picture and what's going to happen in the long run.

Because if everyone just pushes to get his way in the short term, we're all just going to end up getting soaked on a drowning raft.

The castaway kid

Face it, when you see a supervisor striding toward you, eyes locked on yours, mouth drawn tight - any pleasant thoughts flee like a third-grader told to clean his room.

I considered hiding as the supervisor bore down toward me. What could I possibly have done? I was working a parade audience control shift at the Magic Kingdom, for heaven's sake. And the parade wasn't starting for another hour - I was just killing time pretending to keep people from mobbing the turkey leg stand.

"We need you on the rafts, Robert."

What? Tom Sawyer Island closed nearly half an hour ago. I could see the mainland and maintenance docks - all four rafts are tied up and shut down for the night. Why on Earth would we need a raft for now? To film the back of the crowd during the parade?

I followed the supervisor down the exit path toward the rafts' dock. Ahead, flying in from 9 o'clock, I saw two security guards, the area supervisor and, gulp! the park duty manager, all closing in.

Whiskey, Tango, Foxtrot? I'd never seen this many high-level managers without Diamond Horseshoe girls present. And everyone was walking waaaay too fast for this to be good news, whatever it was.

What *was* up?

I turned my head, to look back across the water, and then I saw him. A boy, not more than 10 years old, standing on the Tom Sawyer Island dock.

The island-side dock.

It really happened! We'd always talked about it, those of us who worked the island. But I'd dismissed it as an urban legend, something that never actually occurred.

Did you hear about the kid who got left on the island, after it closed for the night?

This kid had done it. With an effort that Tom Sawyer himself surely would have admired, he'd evaded the security guards who sweep the island each evening at dusk. Somehow, he'd found a way to hide, so he could stay the night on Tom Sawyer Island.

This boy was my hero. The suits kept grim expressions on their faces as I cast off to drive them across the river and pick up our castaway. But my face held a smile as wide as the river itself. Well-played, Tom, Jr.

I steered the raft along a wide left turn toward the island-side dock, drawing close enough to make eye contact with Tom, Jr. for the first time. My smile melted immediately when I saw the fear choking his attempts to breathe. Scared, exhausted, this kid didn't care about paying homage to Tom and Huck. He wasn't playing a game. He wanted off this island, now. The supervisor hollered at him to stay put, when it looked like he might jump from the dock onto the raft, as soon as we sailed near.

I tied up quickly, as the child dashed onto the raft. Safe now; breath came, fueling the sobs he finally could let free. A cast member working a souvenir stand across the river had seen the boy waving for help. Within five minutes, managers across the park had been notified, with one charged to find the nearest available raft driver – which just happened to be me.

The boy had seen the security guard on his closing rounds and had thought it fun to try to hide. He hadn't thought past that.

He'd run around the island, looking for the bridge or pathway back to the parade route, where he was supposed to meet his family. Alone, with no way off the island, he'd returned to the dock and started yelling for help.

As I drove back toward the mainland, more slowly this time, the color returned to the boy's face. Just as it drained from the face of the security supervisor who was taking the report. His guy had blown it - calling the island clear, when it wasn't. And hours of paperwork, and a certain reprimand, would be the price.

We reached the dock and my eyes caught the boy's again. The smile returned to my face as I tried to tell him, with only a look, that everything was all right now. Hey, maybe, months or years from now, when the fear no longer hurt so much, he'd have a cool story to tell:

"Did you hear about the kid who got left on the island, after it closed for the night?"

The day it snowed at Disney World

Even in December, the weather in Central Florida remains pleasant on most days. But once a decade or so, a nasty cold front penetrates the state, freezing orange trees, tourists and even residents.

The morning of December 23, 1989 brought one of those fronts. With the forecast calling for temperatures to fall into the 30s, I hauled my Chicago winter coat from the back of the hall closet. Good that I did, too. Watching other opening-shift cast members shiver in their jean jackets and sweatshirts while I stayed toasty warm, I was glad that I had dressed as someone should for near-freezing temperatures – despite the fact that I now lived in Florida, where the weather wasn't supposed to do this.

That day I was opening at Tom Sawyer Island, driving rafts across the river. We didn't expect much of a crowd. It was Saturday, two days before Christmas. Most people coming down for the holidays would be traveling that day, making it a busy day at the airport, but not at Walt Disney World. (Certainly no local would be fool enough to come out in this weather, either.)

A freeze doesn't come to Central Florida the way it arrives up north, with weeks-long gradual cooling into the 30s and 20s, leaves turning, and warmth slowly escaping the ground. Instead, Arctic air blows sharply into Florida, shrouding the still-warm waters and soil.

What happens when you drop a blanket of Yankee winter air on top of warm Florida water?

You get fog. Lots and lots of dense fog.

Actually, the morning's fog wasn't too bad when I arrived. I drove the crew who worked the snack stand on the island without hassle. No, I couldn't see all the way across Frontierland to the Country Bear Jamboree from the middle of the river, like I could on a clear day, but I could see from the dock on one bank to the other, which was all I really needed.

So we opened the island to a small cluster of shivering guests, stuffed into the winter coats they hadn't expected to be wearing in Florida. Everyone wore their shoulders around their ears that morning.

Then the temperature kept dropping, down through the 30s, on its way to what would be the day's low: in the mid-20s. The fog thickened. As I docked the raft on the mainland side after my second or third crossing, I heard the riverboat's whistle. I turned to signal the riverboat clear... and couldn't see it. Nor could I see across the river to the island dock.

Lake Buena Vista, we've got a problem.

My lead called a supervisor to let him know we were going down, and we learned that we weren't the only ones making the same call. Big Thunder Mountain couldn't open at all, since the ride's trains kept speeding over the frozen track. The fog enveloping Tom Sawyer Island had also covered the Seven Seas Lagoon, taking down the ferryboats and forcing all guests to access the Magic Kingdom via monorail. The Jungle Cruise was down, too. As was People Mover, Dumbo and just about every other outdoor ride in the park.

But we still had about a dozen guests on the island. The riverboat would have to dock while I ferried over a security guard to help the rest of the Tom Sawyer Island crew clear the island. Frankly, the guests seemed happy to go. Half of them already had gathered on the dock for the return trip. The rest we found huddled in one of the caves, trying to stay warm.

No one stepped up to relieve me of raft-driving duties. (Gee, I wonder why?) So I sailed blind through the muck on that final trip back to the mainland. Cocky raft drivers say that they can make the trip blind. I got to prove it.

When we arrived, two of my friends from other attractions were waiting for me. With half the rides in the park closed, leads were releasing any cast members who wanted to leave early. Rather than spend the day shivering at the entrance to the Tom Sawyer Island queue, just to let people know that they couldn't visit an island they could no longer see, I took an early release, too.

We decided we'd go play in the park – but somewhere indoors. We chose The Land pavilion at Epcot, which, we would later discover, had become the most popular destination in all of Walt Disney World that day, with crowds thicker than the fog.

On my way over to the tunnels to change clothes and clock out, I felt something fly into my eye. A bug? I blinked instinctually, and my brought my hand to my eye to wipe away whatever it was. Then I felt the offending speck melt to water instead. No way! Standing in the middle of Frontierland, I looked to the sky and saw... snowflakes.

It was snowing... at Walt Disney World.

My Christmas morning at Walt Disney World

The two kids flew by me, running through the Pirates of the Caribbean turnstiles, moments after seven in the morning.

Dad, with his newly-bought coffee in hand, lingered in the plaza. The morning air felt bitterly cold, after the snow earlier that week.

"Merry Christmas," I told him, the first of many such greetings I'd be offering that day.

"Merry Christmas," he replied, stamping his feet. Few tourists had brought the right clothes for the cold snap. "Wow, it must be tough working Christmas morning."

I laughed.

"Actually," I said, "several of us were just wondering if we'd find anyone out here coming to Disney World first thing on Christmas morning."

To be honest, I think the actual words another Pirates cast member had used moments before the park opened were something like, "I cannot believe that anyone in their right mind would come to Disney World instead of spending Christmas morning opening presents." But I didn't tell the Dad that.

He laughed.

"Yeah, you'd think that we'd be opening presents somewhere, right?"

The guy reads minds, I guessed. Another family walked into the plaza, shivering as they pushed through the turnstiles.

"Well, obviously I'm skipping that, too," I said with a grin. Of course, I'd be opening presents with my family before Christmas dinner that afternoon, after my shift, so it wasn't like I wasn't going to be celebrating the day. I wondered if they'd be doing something similar, too, later in the day at whatever hotel where they were staying.

The Dad's focus shifted; he turned his eyes from me toward the passageway his kids had run into.

"The kids said they really wanted to go to Disney World for Christmas," he said. "Their mom and I told them that we couldn't afford that, with other presents, too."

He sipped his coffee.

"So the kids said, 'Fine, let's skip the other presents and all give each other a trip to Disney World, instead,'" he continued.

The Dad brought his eyes back to me, and I could see a misty look in them, one that had nothing to do with the cold.

"So I guess they're opening their presents now, after all."

He stood, silently now, with a silly grin on his face, his eyes drifting back down the passageway.

I let him have the moment, then spoke.

"They'll be exiting through the shops over to your right, sir," I said.

"Oh... yes. Thanks."

"Sir?"

He looked back at me, as he walked across the plaza.

"Merry Christmas," I said.

The most money I ever made working at Disney

Seven hours before, I had been jammed in the middle of a swarm of tens of thousands of people, watching explosions fill the sky around us. Many in the swarm tried to hug the friends and family who surrounded them, but failed. Those friends and family stood so close, few could raise their arms. Limbs useless, people used their voices instead, screaming, "Happy New Year!" until enough people on the periphery of the swarm had moved, giving us somewhere to go.

Now, in morning light, I stood just yards away from that place, but alone.

No voices. No explosions. I could spread my arms as wide as I could stretch them. I was alone, driving a raft around the Rivers of America in the country's most popular theme park - now empty, just hours after the moment during the year when it is most filled.

I wasn't supposed to be the opening lead at Tom Sawyer Island on that New Year's morning. But all the other raft-driving leads were at that moment unconscious, with lingering blood alcohol levels that would have landed them multiple court dates had they been behind the wheel of a car. Instead, they had wisely chosen to remain crashed on various beds, couches and floors around the Orlando metro area.

And thus, I got the gig.

My wife, a musician, insists that violins retain a physical memory of the music that's been played upon them. Her thoughts prompted me to wonder if theme parks don't in some way retain a similar energy from the crowds who visit. Certainly, there's an energy to the design of parks, one that's intended to infuse visitors with anticipation and excitement.

With no one else in sight on an early morning, all that energy flows through just one person - you. You might think that being alone in a theme park would leave you with a feeling of calm, even serenity.

Nope, with all that energy flowing toward me, and me alone... well, I felt giddier than I ever had before in the Magic Kingdom.

Of course, the math I was doing in my head at that moment probably added to my excitement. As a full-time employee, I was earning pay for a full eight-hour shift that holiday whether I worked or not. And since I was working a lead shift, I was earning an extra $2.50 a hour for the eight hours I would be working that day.

But that wasn't the best part. Since less than six hours had passed between the end of my Parade Audience Control shift at 1:30 that morning and the start of my leads shift at 7 am, I started the day on the same pay rate which I'd ended the shift before. And since I'd picked up the extra parade shift after my scheduled raft-driving shift yesterday... I was earning double-time.

Lead double-time.

With holiday pay.

Meaning that I was earning almost four times my normal hourly pay, to drive a raft around Tom Sawyer Island in an empty Magic Kingdom, as the creatures and characters of my beloved Rivers of America staged a private show, just for me.

Thank you to Disney's labor unions for making that a very happy new year, indeed.

An unexpected gift

If you pressed me to name my favorite perk I earned working at Walt Disney World, I'd have to say... the free tickets. When I worked full-time at the Mouse House, I had a pass that I could use to sign in a certain number of family and friends 12 times a year. But even part-timers got the company-wide gift of free Disney tickets twice a year - around Christmas and the Fourth of July.

As a single person with no kids (back then), I got two tickets each time. But these were no ordinary free tickets. They were one-day park-hoppers, then unavailable to the general public. And not only were they good at all the Walt Disney World theme parks, they were good at Disneyland, as well. (Which prompted just about everyone to wonder if we could run around to all the Disney World parks in the morning, drive to Orlando International Airport, hop a flight to Los Angeles and bag Disneyland the same day, on the same ticket. Of course, we figured, anyone who could afford the plane ticket probably could have afforded their own Disney tickets anyway.)

I hoarded these tickets, amassing a decent pile over the summer and winter holidays I worked while in college and graduate school. They came in handy later, when I was a broke journalism graduate student, as they made excellent wedding presents for the many friends who got hitched when I was in my mid-20s and had no extra cash to buy decent presents.

But one of my fellow cast members didn't wait to make a gift of her tickets. She was in school, too, and had collected quite a few free tickets as she'd been working at Disney since high school. After our shifts had ended in the Magic Kingdom one July day, we'd ridden the monorail over to Epcot for a cast-discount dinner at Epcot's Le Cellier Restaurant. (This was back in the days before Priority Seating, when it was possible to get a table at Le Cellier without weeks of advance notice.)

On our way back, she'd struck up a conversation with a couple of kids about their day at Disney. They were having a great time, and were gushing to my co-worker about everything they'd seen. After a few moments, they started pestering their mother if they could stay another day.

"No, kids," the mother explained patiently. "Our tickets are up today, and we're going to go to the beach tomorrow."

As she said this, I saw my co-worker reach into her purse. She pulled out the free tickets she'd just gotten and - to my shock - handed them over to the mom.

"I work in the Magic Kingdom," my co-worker explained. "And Disney gives us free tickets every now and then. I don't need them - I can get into the park for free whenever I want - and it seems like your kids are having such a good time. Here - I want you to have them."

The mother looked stunned. "No, I..." was all she could get out.

"I insist," my co-worker said, as the kids squealed.

The monorail arrived at the Magic Kingdom, and my co-worker got up to exit before the mom could refuse. "Thank you," the mom said to my co-worker, who simply smiled in return. I collected my jaw from the floor and ran after my co-worker.

I was going to ask, "Why?" but when I saw the smile on her face and the joy she exuded... I had my answer.

Sometimes, you find the greatest joy not in what you get or what you achieve, but in what you do for other people. Even people you do not know, and who never would have expected it.

When you're no longer a cast member

At what point do you stop being cast member?

Sure, there's the last day at work in the parks. But not always. My last summer at the Magic Kingdom, I worked as a seasonal employee, pulling weekend shifts at Tom Sawyer Island and weeknight shifts at parade audience control. (On weekdays, I was working as a news intern for Orlando's big news/talk radio station.) I didn't take special note of my final shift as a Disney World cast member because I hadn't thought it would be my last. My plan was to come back from graduate journalism school and work the Christmas holidays at Disney. But the local newspaper up in Indiana hired me instead, so I called in and quit my Disney job, to start my journalism career.

But in some sense, I never stopped acting a cast member, even after that day when I quit. Obviously, my love for theme parks has endured, and I continue to use ThemeParkInsider.com to help people get the most from their theme park visits, just as I did (in a far more limited way) working inside the parks.

When I visit the parks themselves, whether I am at the Magic Kingdom or another Disney park, I still find myself... slipping into the cast member role. On my daughter's recent birthday at Disneyland, I chased down one of the Main Street Vehicles to return two hats to a mother and daughter, after they'd blown off in the street in front of me. Later, at Small World, I smiled silently at an older woman whose friend was fumbling with a camera while trying to take a group picture. The woman asked her friend to hand me the camera, and I took the picture, with everyone included. A couple of lost guests stopped to ask me questions. I picked up a piece of trash from the street. Five summers of working in the Magic Kingdom taught me habits that I, obviously, have yet to break.

You know what? I'm happy with that. Creating magic is really just about creating a friendly environment where people are always ready to help one another. At one point, that was my job, and Disney paid me to do it. Today, with ThemeParkInsider.com, it's still my job, even though my paycheck comes from another source.

Maybe some people never stop acting a cast member - at least not entirely. Thank goodness for that.

About the Author

Robert Niles is the founder and editor of ThemeParkInsider.com, an online consumers' guide to the world's leading theme and amusement parks, read by more than 200,000 people each month. It has been named the top theme park site on the Internet by *Forbes* and *Travel + Leisure* magazines, and is a Webby Award finalist and winner of the Online Journalism Award, presented by the Online News Association and the Columbia Graduate School of Journalism.

Robert worked at Walt Disney's World Magic Kingdom for five summers between 1987 and 1991, as well as for a full year between graduating Northwestern University and beginning graduate school in journalism at Indiana University. In the years since leaving Disney, Robert's worked as a reporter, editorial writer, columnist and website editor for several newspapers, including *The* [Bloomington, Indiana] *Herald-Times*, the *Omaha* [Nebraska] *World-Herald*, the [Denver] *Rocky Mountain News* and the *Los Angeles Times*.

Robert is a native of Los Angeles and today lives in Pasadena, California with his wife and two children.

You can follow ThemeParkInsider.com on the Internet at **www.themeparkinsider.com**.

 We're also on Facebook at
www.facebook.com/themeparkinsider

 And Twitter at **twitter.com/themepark**

16883884R00080

Made in the USA
Lexington, KY
18 August 2012